DYNAMIC
DEFENSE

by Mike Lawrence
Edited by Bernie Yomtov

Published by
Devyn Press
Louisville, Kentucky

Cover by Bonnie Baron Pollack

Printed in the United States of America.

Baron Barclay Bridge Supply
3600 Chamberlain Lane, Suite 206
Louisville, KY 40241
1-800-274-2221

Fifth Printing

ISBN 0-910791-01-5

Introduction

There are many good books on defense which present hands in problem form. The reader is led to the crucial point of the hand, and must decide what to do. He is then shown the author's analysis of the hand. The problem with this approach is twofold. First of all, the reader knows when the problem comes, which is not the case at the bridge table. Secondly, the reader is left on his own to develop the thought processes necessary to solve the problem.

In this book, Mike takes a different approach. During the bidding you are only shown one hand, as in real life, and he lucidly explains his thoughts about each bid as the auction proceeds and the opening lead is made. When the dummy appears, he verbalizes his thinking in appraising the defence's chances and planning the defense in exactly the same way an expert would approach the hand at the table. The clues about the hand are compiled trick by trick, until the moment of truth arrives. At all points Lawrence is explaining the expert's thinking process as the hand unfolds, so the reader can understand how the expert comes to the proper conclusions. At the end of the hand, there is an analysis of the deal and of any points of interest regarding the hand.

While this book can be read solely for enjoyment, the ambitious reader will find it very instructive. He should stop at each point in the bidding and play, form his own analyses and conclusions, and then compare them to Lawrence's. In this way, the reader can see weaknesses in his own thinking process, and improve his planning of the defense of a hand.

It is not often that one can sit next to an expert and have the expert explain exactly what he is thinking at each point in the bidding and play. This is exactly what Mike has done, and any bridge player will enjoy the book while improving his defense, regardless of his skill level.

Kit Woolsey

1

♠ A 8 3
♡ J 9 2
◇ J 9 6
♣ J 7 3 2

With no one vulnerable, West deals and bids ONE NO-TRUMP. East raises to TWO NOTRUMP and West continues to THREE NOTRUMP. I check their notrump range. It is fifteen to seventeen.

Dealer: West
Vul: None

WEST	NORTH	EAST	SOUTH
1 NT	Pass	2 NT	Pass
3 NT	Pass	Pass	Pass

Partner leads the king of spades and dummy appears:

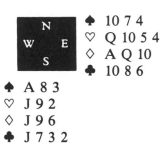

♠ 10 7 4
♡ Q 10 5 4
◇ A Q 10
♣ 10 8 6

♠ A 8 3
♡ J 9 2
◇ J 9 6
♣ J 7 3 2

It looks like we are off to a good start and I encourage with the eight. When partner continues with the Queen I have to decide whether to overtake, playing partner for KQJx(x), or to duck, playing partner for KQx.

Can I tell what is right?

Yes. There is a useful convention which solves this problem.

When you lead from an honor sequence and hold the trick, your next play should be the lowest remaining honor in your sequence. With KQJxx, you lead the king and continue with the jack. With KQx you lead the king and continue with the queen.

I therefore know that partner's lead is from KQx, so I must play the three. Partner can't tell from my play that I have only three spades so he continues with the five to my ace. Declarer has followed with three small ones, so the jack is still missing. I am quite confident that we have just established it for declarer. At least we have not established two tricks for him.

Partner also knows that declarer has the jack of spades, since I would have won the third trick with the jack, not the ace, if my original holding had been AJ83.

How can we set this contract?

Is it possible we have two fast tricks? Can partner have the ace and king of hearts or the ace and queen of clubs?

No. Partner can have only eight or nine points, and has already shown up with five. He probably has one more significant high card.

Since we aren't going to beat three notrump immediately, I'm going to look for as safe an exit as possible.

Which suit is safest?

Hearts are dangerous. If declarer has the ace, a heart shift will spare him a guess. And if declarer has the king, a heart lead will concede an otherwise impossible trick.

Diamonds are quite safe. There is no holding where a diamond lead will cost a trick.

Clubs are dangerous, although not as dangerous as hearts. If declarer holds AQx(x), he can duck my lead to the ten and end up with two or three club tricks. If I don't open up this suit, he may take only one. On this particular hand clubs are not so dangerous. If partner has the ace or king, or even the king and queen of clubs, declarer will have nine tricks, one spade, four hearts, three diamonds and one club, and will not need a second club trick.

I choose to lead the diamond six. Declarer wins with dummy's ten and leads a heart to his king. Partner produces the ace and eventually I win the setting trick with the heart jack.

The complete hand:

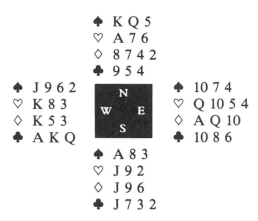

```
                ♠ K Q 5
                ♡ A 7 6
                ◇ 8 7 4 2
                ♣ 9 5 4
♠ J 9 6 2            N            ♠ 10 7 4
♡ K 8 3        W         E        ♡ Q 10 5 4
◇ K 5 3            S            ◇ A Q 10
♣ A K Q                          ♣ 10 8 6
                ♠ A 8 3
                ♡ J 9 2
                ◇ J 9 6
                ♣ J 7 3 2
```

Now that the hand is over, I wonder why East didn't bid Stayman. Even though he had a balanced hand there is no reason that West couldn't have had four hearts with a weak holding in either clubs or spades.

FURTHER ANALYSIS

The conventional treatment I have described here can be extended to other combinations:

KQJx(x)   Lead the king, follow with the jack
KQx   Lead the king, follow with the queen
KQxx(x)   If you chose to lead the king, follow with the fourth best
QJ10x(x) Lead the queen, follow with the ten
QJx   Lead the queen, follow with the jack
J109x(x) Lead the jack, follow with the nine
J10x   Lead the jack, follow with the ten

One of the more embarrassing things a defender can do is unblock a suit and then find out it was declarer's suit and not partner's. I know of more than one instance where very good defenders did just this.

Note that it is important to consider whether a passive defense is called for. Often, your goal should be to exit safely rather than to make a risky play with little or no chance of success.

2

♠ Q 5
♡ A Q 5
♢ K Q 9 8 7
♣ A K 8

With our opponents vulnerable, my partner passes. I might consider opening two notrump, but before I can do that, East opens ONE SPADE. I DOUBLE and West raises to TWO SPADES. This hand is not as good as it looks, but when the auction gets passed back to me, I DOUBLE again. Partner responds THREE DIAMONDS. Surprisingly, opener contests with THREE SPADES. With no overwhelming sense of security, I raise to FOUR DIAMONDS. When it gets back to opener, he discovers something he's overlooked before and tries FOUR SPADES. Things have gone far enough and I DOUBLE again. Even allowing for no diamond tricks, I have four potential tricks in hearts and clubs. The queen of spades may also take a trick.

This has been the complete auction:

Dealer: North
Vul: East-West

NORTH	EAST	SOUTH	WEST
Pass	1 ♠	Double	2 ♠
Pass	Pass	Double	Pass
3 ♢	3 ♠	4 ♢	Pass
Pass	4 ♠	Double	Pass
Pass	Pass	Pass	

I lead the king of clubs and dummy tables:

♠ A 9 6
♡ 10 7 4 3
◊ 6 5
♣ Q J 7 6

♠ Q 5
♡ A Q 5
◊ K Q 9 8 7
♣ A K 8

At trick one, partner plays the two. I switch to the diamond king and partner plays the jack. I take this to show the ten. Given the auction, partner is not likely to have another high card let alone the ace of diamonds.

Declarer takes the ace of diamonds and plays the king followed by the jack of spades. There goes my hope of scoring the queen of spades. Partner follows twice to spades, playing the four and the eight.

Declarer now ruffs dummy's remaining diamond and leads the ten of clubs. I must decide whether to win this and if I win, how to continue.

Is it possible that partner's jack of diamonds was suit preference for hearts? Does he have the heart king?

No. His diamond play did not show the heart king. In the first place he can't have it. And in the second place he was showing the ten of diamonds which, from his point of view, might provide a crucial entry to his hand. As a general rule, suit preference takes a back seat to other defensive signals.

How many tricks does declarer have? What does this imply?

He has only nine tricks outside hearts: six spades, one diamond, and two clubs. Consequently he will still have to lose two hearts after discarding on the fourth club. So the winning play is to take the club ace and play another club, and wait for my two heart tricks.

The complete hand:

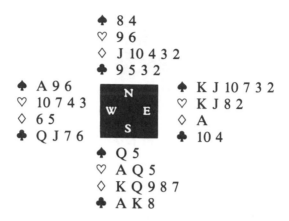

```
                  ♠ 8 4
                  ♡ 9 6
                  ◇ J 10 4 3 2
                  ♣ 9 5 3 2
   ♠ A 9 6                        ♠ K J 10 7 3 2
   ♡ 10 7 4 3        N            ♡ K J 8 2
   ◇ 6 5         W       E        ◇ A
   ♣ Q J 7 6         S            ♣ 10 4
                  ♠ Q 5
                  ♡ A Q 5
                  ◇ K Q 9 8 7
                  ♣ A K 8
```

FURTHER ANALYSIS

Partner's play of the club deuce at trick one discouraged a club continuation, fulfilling his first obligation, and did not show count.

Note declarer's play of ruffing out the diamonds before conceding the second club. It gave a careless defense the chance to do the wrong thing. Also note declarer's bidding. It is characteristic of some players that they visualize perfect cards in their partner's hand. The three spade bid was aggressive, but well judged. The four spade bid, though, was atrocious. Declarer was hoping for something like four spades to the ace and the queen of hearts in dummy. But if he was going to hope for that, he should have made a game try two rounds earlier.

3

♠ Q J
♡ Q 6 5
◇ Q 7 6 2
♣ A 10 5 4

With no one vulnerable I am the dealer and I pass. West opens ONE SPADE. When East responds ONE NOTRUMP, I pass again. The auction continues with TWO HEARTS by opener and a preference to TWO SPADES by responder. This is passed out and partner leads the queen of clubs.

Dealer: South
Vul: None

SOUTH	WEST	NORTH	EAST
Pass	1 ♠	Pass	1 NT
Pass	2 ♡	Pass	2 ♠
Pass	Pass	Pass	

```
            N            ♠ 10 7 3
       W         E       ♡ K 9 4
            S            ◇ 9 4 3
                         ♣ K 9 6 3
         ♠ Q J
         ♡ Q 6 5
         ◇ Q 7 6 2
         ♣ A 10 5 4
```

When dummy plays the three, I encourage with the five. Declarer follows with the eight. Partner eventually continues with the jack of clubs. Dummy and I play low and declarer ruffs with the spade two. He continues with the spade four to partner's nine, dummy's ten and my jack. How should I continue?

It doesn't look right to lead a club, and hearts are certainly dangerous. The queen of spades is safe enough, but it feels more natural to lead a diamond.

Is a diamond right?

It might be, but that nine of diamonds is somewhat threatening. If declarer has K10x, then a diamond lead gives him a trick which he could not get for himself. If he has AJ10 or KJ10, I will be playing a suit for him which he has insufficient entries to play himself. My queen of hearts suggests he may have to take a heart finesse and his only apparent entry is the king of hearts.

How many diamonds does declarer have?

Declarer has probably got five spades, four hearts, one club and therefore three diamonds.

If declarer has three diamonds, and I choose to lead the queen of spades, will our diamond tricks go away?

No. Declarer might discard one diamond from dummy on a heart, but we will still get in with a diamond in time to draw dummy's third spade. Declarer will not be able to ruff his diamond loser in dummy. If declarer has AKx of diamonds and AJxx of hearts we cannot win a diamond trick by any defense.

Is there a case where leading the spade queen will cost a trick?

Yes. If declarer has:

♠ Axxxx
♡ AJxxx
♢ Ax
♣ x

he will be able to discard two diamonds from dummy on his hearts and then get his diamond ruff. If this is the actual layout, I must return a diamond.

Which is more likely?

I think it is far more likely that declarer is 5-4-3-1 and I am going to defend on this assumption. I return the spade queen and declarer looks annoyed. If this annoyance is justified then I have done the right thing. Declarer wins the spade return with the ace, partner following with the eight. Now comes the king of hearts, a heart finesse to the jack, and two more hearts, discarding a diamond from dummy. Partner refrains from trumping the fourth heart and declarer eventually loses three diamonds and another spade.

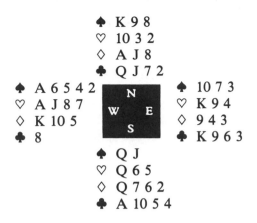

                    ♠ K 9 8
                    ♡ 10 3 2
                    ◇ A J 8
                    ♣ Q J 7 2
    ♠ A 6 5 4 2   ♠ 10 7 3
    ♡ A J 8 7   ♡ K 9 4
    ◇ K 10 5   ◇ 9 4 3
    ♣ 8   ♣ K 9 6 3
                    ♠ Q J
                    ♡ Q 6 5
                    ◇ Q 7 6 2
                    ♣ A 10 5 4

FURTHER ANALYSIS

Frequently it is best for defenders not to open up new suits, even when it seems obvious to do so. When it is evident that declarer will have to play a suit eventually you should leave him to his own devices if possible.

4

♠ Q 4 3
♡ A 9 3 2
◊ K 2
♣ 6 5 4 2

With the opponents vulnerable, there are three passes to my LHO who opens ONE SPADE. RHO responds ONE NOTRUMP. When opener rebids TWO HEARTS his partner returns to TWO SPADES. I comment that this auction sounds familiar. Indeed it is. It is identical to the previous one.

Dealer: North
Vul: East-West

NORTH	EAST	SOUTH	WEST
Pass	Pass	Pass	1 ♠
Pass	1 NT	Pass	2 ♡
Pass	2 ♠	Pass	Pass
Pass			

However partner's lead is not identical. It is a rather surprising eight of hearts. Dummy appears and I have to sort out a somewhat unusual problem.

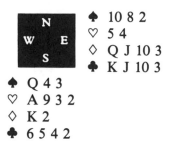

♠ 10 8 2
♡ 5 4
◊ Q J 10 3
♣ K J 10 3

♠ Q 4 3
♡ A 9 3 2
◊ K 2
♣ 6 5 4 2

On the auction you would expect partner to lead one of the unbid suits more often than not, and a case could be made for a trump lead. But a heart lead! Most peculiar. It doesn't look like a singleton. Did partner hear the bidding?

Why would partner lead a heart? Assuming that partner does know how the bidding went, and that he is not looking for a heart ruff, then it stands to reason that partner has led a heart because his other choices were worse. Since he would prefer to lead a minor suit on this auction, he must have strong reasons not to, and these reasons can only be that he holds both minor suit aces. Even a trump lead would normally have more to recommend it than a heart, so he probably has some trump holding such as Kx or Jx.

How should the defense proceed?

Since I trust partner not to lead a heart without a sound reason I'm going to defend on the assumption that I can tell why partner has made this unusual lead.

I win the heart ace and switch to the king of diamonds. It will not take long to see if my reasoning is accurate. Declarer plays the six and my partner the eight. So far, so good. I continue with the two to partner's ace. He returns the four which I ruff, declarer following. I take partner's four to be suit preference for clubs, confirming my original hypothesis. Partner takes my club return with ace and plays another diamond. I ruff this with the queen. Declarer overruffs but the uppercut has worked. Partner wins the trump jack for down one.

The complete hand is as anticipated:

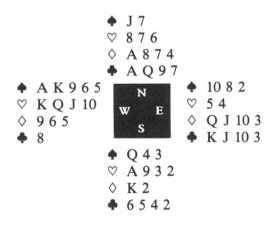

```
                    ♠ J 7
                    ♡ 8 7 6
                    ◇ A 8 7 4
                    ♣ A Q 9 7
     ♠ A K 9 6 5        N        ♠ 10 8 2
     ♡ K Q J 10                  ♡ 5 4
     ◇ 9 6 5       W        E    ◇ Q J 10 3
     ♣ 8              S          ♣ K J 10 3
                    ♠ Q 4 3
                    ♡ A 9 3 2
                    ◇ K 2
                    ♣ 6 5 4 2
```

FURTHER ANALYSIS

If partner had five diamonds, and declarer two, partner would cash the club ace and then:
1. exit with a club or
2. exit with a diamond, expecting you to ruff as high as possible. On the actual hand, I was sure that declarer had a third diamond.

If you are doubtful about the analysis, look at partner's hand and see how you feel about your choice of leads.

Compare the hand with one of these:

♠ K J
♥ 8 7 6
♦ 9 8 5 4   Wouldn't you lead a diamond?
♣ A Q 9 7

    or

♠ K J
♥ 8 7 6
♦ A 9 8 5   Wouldn't you prefer to lead a club?
♣ Q 9 8 7

The point is that partner's heart lead could be identified as a least of evils lead. He probably didn't like leading hearts, but his other choices were worse.

5

♠ K 7 6
♡ A J 6 5
◇ 8 7 2
♣ J 9 5

With both sides vulnerable, RHO deals and opens ONE DIA-
MOND. LHO responds ONE HEART and opener rebids TWO
DIAMONDS. LHO's THREE NOTRUMP ends the auction
and partner leads the three of spades.

Dealer: East
Vul: Both

EAST	SOUTH	WEST	NORTH
1 ◇	Pass	1 ♡	Pass
2 ◇	Pass	3 NT	Pass
Pass	Pass		

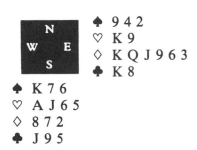

♠ 9 4 2
♡ K 9
◇ K Q J 9 6 3
♣ K 8

♠ K 7 6
♡ A J 6 5
◇ 8 7 2
♣ J 9 5

I play the king and declarer considers momentarily before
taking the ace. He follows with the ten of diamonds which holds
the trick. I'm pretty sure partner has the ace of diamonds
though. In any case, if he doesn't have it, we are unlikely to beat
three notrump. For us to succeed, partner must have good
spades, plus the ace of diamonds. And if partner's spades require a lead from my side of the table, he will have to find my
entry.

I'm going to try to tell partner my entry is in hearts.

How can I do that?

The one thing I can't do is to play the eight of diamonds on
the first round of diamonds. Partner would take that as a count

signal showing the number of diamonds I held. Instead, I play the two. When declarer continues diamonds, I play the eight. Since partner knows I have three of them, he will interpret my play as showing good hearts. He is not bound to lead a heart, but the information may be of use to him.

On this hand the information is of use, and when partner produces the ace of diamonds, he switches to the seven of hearts. When I return the seven of spades, partner is able to cash three spades.

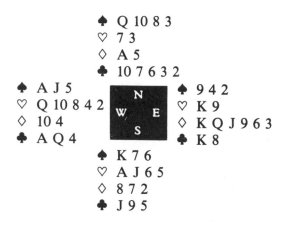

♠ Q 10 8 3
♡ 7 3
◇ A 5
♣ 10 7 6 3 2

♠ A J 5
♡ Q 10 8 4 2
◇ 10 4
♣ A Q 4

♠ 9 4 2
♡ K 9
◇ K Q J 9 6 3
♣ K 8

♠ K 7 6
♡ A J 6 5
◇ 8 7 2
♣ J 9 5

FURTHER ANALYSIS

Had partner taken the first diamond, there would be some merit to playing the eight as suit preference. This is because the count signal would have diminished value. This is a delicate area however, and unless clearly understood, it is usually better to give priority to count or attitude signals over suit preference signals.

6

♠ Q 9 3
♡ A Q J 10
◇ Q
♣ 9 8 7 6 4

Vul vs not, my RHO opens with ONE DIAMOND. It is tempting to take some action. Double is possible and I might consider one heart, but being vulnerable I choose discretion and pass. When LHO responds ONE HEART I feel better about my pass. Opener rebids ONE SPADE and responder ends the auction with THREE NOTRUMP.

Dealer: East
Vul: North-South

EAST	SOUTH	WEST	NORTH
1 ◇	Pass	1 ♡	Pass
1 ♠	Pass	3 NT	Pass
Pass	Pass		

Partner leads the jack of clubs.

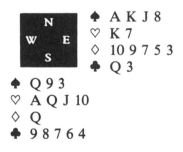

♠ A K J 8
♡ K 7
◇ 10 9 7 5 3
♣ Q 3

♠ Q 9 3
♡ A Q J 10
◇ Q
♣ 9 8 7 6 4

Dummy wins the first trick with the queen, and since I desperately want a heart shift, I play the four of clubs.

Declarer leads a small diamond to my queen and his ace. He follows with the jack of diamonds which wins. I think my partner has the diamond king and is holding up. If he doesn't have it, we are in trouble. In any event, I must find a discard or two. What shall I discard?

I would like to tell partner to shift to a heart, but I hate to signal with a heart because it would be at the expense of one of my heart tricks. The classic case of signalling with the setting trick. Nor does it look right to throw a spade. I'm going to part with the six of clubs. Declarer now leads a third diamond and partner finally produces the king. Now if I can get a heart shift, we can beat three notrump. I wonder. If I throw a heart and get partner to lead one, can I effectively shift back to clubs.

Will this work?

I think that declarer is marked with the ace and king of clubs from his jump to three notrump. He has nothing in spades or hearts, so the only points he can have are the ace and jack of diamonds and the ace and king of clubs, a twelve count. If we were playing that the lead of a jack denies a higher honor, I would know this for sure.

Since this is my last chance to persuade partner to lead hearts, I better find a way if there is one. I think partner should lead one in any case, but he might decide three notrump is cold and defend passively to hold down overtricks.

Is there a winning discard?

I could play the three of spades hoping partner will appreciate my interest in hearts, but I think I can do better. I discard the queen of spades. If this doesn't get a heart lead nothing will. Partner looks at this with a little surprise as does declarer. When partner leads the heart six, I am able to take four tricks for down one.

The entire hand:

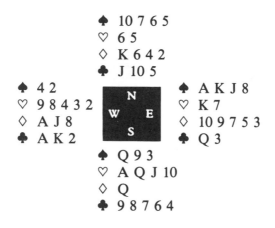

```
                  ♠ 10 7 6 5
                  ♡ 6 5
                  ◇ K 6 4 2
                  ♣ J 10 5
     ♠ 4 2                        ♠ A K J 8
     ♡ 9 8 4 3 2       N          ♡ K 7
     ◇ A J 8        W     E       ◇ 10 9 7 5 3
     ♣ A K 2           S          ♣ Q 3
                  ♠ Q 9 3
                  ♡ A Q J 10
                  ◇ Q
                  ♣ 9 8 7 6 4
```

FURTHER ANALYSIS

Generally speaking, it is very difficult to give preference for the lower ranking suit. Small cards which you would like to use as suit preference usually mean attitude. The nine of spades would have been come-on for spades. Only the queen will get a heart shift. Note also that you couldn't afford the spade queen until partner won the diamond trick. If you had thrown the spade queen earlier you might have given declarer his ninth trick.

♠ A K J 8 6
♡ A 8 4
◇ 8
♣ Q 10 3 2

Vul vs not, I finally get a good hand. I open ONE SPADE
with some anticipation. But it is not to be. Both LHO and partner pass and RHO reopens with TWO HEARTS. It is far too
dangerous to continue with this hand and I pass. LHO wastes
no time going to FOUR HEARTS and everyone passes.

Dealer: South
Vul: North-South

SOUTH	WEST	NORTH	EAST
1 ♠	Pass	Pass	2 ♡
Pass	4 ♡	Pass	Pass
Pass			

I lead the king of spades.

♠ Q 10 4 3 2
♡ K J 7
◇ A J 5 3
♣ J

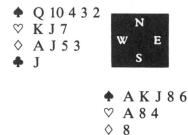

♠ A K J 8 6
♡ A 8 4
◇ 8
♣ Q 10 3 2

This wins as partner plays the five and declarer the seven.
How should I continue?
I can try one of a number of things. I can lead a small trump
or I can lead ace and a trump. I can lead my stiff diamond.
Perhaps partner has the ace of clubs and can give me a diamond
ruff.
Is one of these substantially better than the others?

Yes. There is a best play and it is so good that it is almost one hundred percent. At trick two I shift to the diamond eight. What makes this such a good play?

My intention is to lead my stiff diamond, win the heart ace as soon as possible, and put partner in to give me a diamond ruff. How does partner get in to do this? The key here is the spade partner played at trick one. It was the five. The missing spade is the nine. We have the agreement that we automatically give count in situations such as this. If partner had the nine-five doubleton he would have no choice but to play the nine. Therefore, from his play of five, I know that he, and not declarer, has a singleton spade. I intend to put him in with a spade ruff and get my diamond ruff in return. The reason this play is not a one hundred percent certainty is not that I don't trust partner to have a stiff spade. Rather it is that partner may also have a stiff heart and not be able to ruff the spade, or, rather unlikely, declarer may also have a stiff diamond.

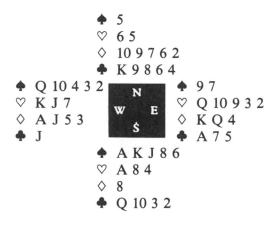

```
              ♠ 5
              ♡ 6 5
              ◊ 10 9 7 6 2
              ♣ K 9 8 6 4
♠ Q 10 4 3 2                    ♠ 9 7
♡ K J 7          N             ♡ Q 10 9 3 2
◊ A J 5 3      W   E           ◊ K Q 4
♣ J              S             ♣ A 7 5
              ♠ A K J 8 6
              ♡ A 8 4
              ◊ 8
              ♣ Q 10 3 2
```

FURTHER ANALYSIS

The important point of this hand is the agreement to give count. You won't always know the distribution. If partner had played the nine, you would not have known if it was a singleton or a doubleton. But if you follow the rule, it will be a big advantage when you *are* able to read partner's card.

8

♠ 7 2
♡ 10 7 5 4 3
♢ A K 2
♣ A Q 4

Vul vs not I open with ONE HEART. Partner raises to TWO HEARTS and RHO overcalls with TWO SPADES. I play that three hearts would be competitive only but this is not the kind of hand for this action, so I pass. LHO bids TWO NOTRUMP but RHO signs off in THREE SPADES.

Dealer: South
Vul: North-South

SOUTH	WEST	NORTH	EAST
1 ♡	Pass	2 ♡	2 ♠
Pass	2 NT	Pass	3 ♠
Pass	Pass	Pass	

I lead the diamond king and quite a good dummy comes down.

♠ K 10 6
♡ K 8 6
♢ Q J 6 5
♣ K J 9

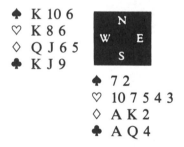

♠ 7 2
♡ 10 7 5 4 3
♢ A K 2
♣ A Q 4

Partner plays the nine so it is easy to continue with the ace. Partner follows with the four and ruffs the third round. He returns the eight of clubs to my ace. There is nothing to do now except return a heart, hoping partner has the ace.

Is this really all there is?

Yes. The real question is which heart to lead.

I do not want partner to play the jack with the AJx of hearts,

24

so I return the heart ten. When dummy plays low, partner looks it over and eventually takes his ace. This turns out to have been necessary.

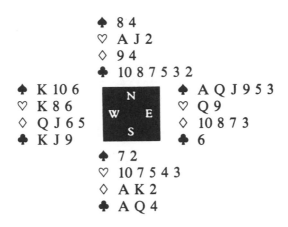

```
                      ♠ 8 4
                      ♡ A J 2
                      ◊ 9 4
                      ♣ 10 8 7 5 3 2
        ♠ K 10 6          N          ♠ A Q J 9 5 3
        ♡ K 8 6      W         E      ♡ Q 9
        ◊ Q J 6 5                     ◊ 10 8 7 3
        ♣ K J 9          S           ♣ 6
                      ♠ 7 2
                      ♡ 10 7 5 4 3
                      ◊ A K 2
                      ♣ A Q 4
```

FURTHER ANALYSIS

There were a lot of good decisions on this hand. Both opponents judged the auction well. Dummy, with a thirteen count, did not stick it in a hopeless game.

Note that when South led the third round of diamonds, it was the deuce. In this instance, it was the only one he had but North couldn't know that and would tend to treat it as suit preference. On this hand that suited South fine and the defense went smoothly. If, however, South's third diamond were the ten, then he might consider the consequences of leading it if he felt partner would do something bad, based on the ten being suit preference.

For instance:

WEST	NORTH	EAST	SOUTH
1 ♡	Pass	2 ♡	2 ♠
Pass	2 NT	Pass	3 ♠
Pass	Pass	Pass	

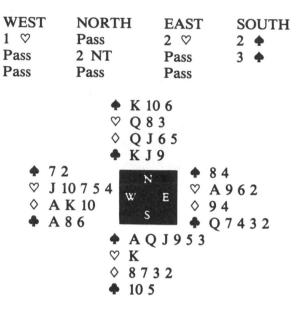

```
                    ♠ K 10 6
                    ♡ Q 8 3
                    ◇ Q J 6 5
                    ♣ K J 9
        ♠ 7 2              N        ♠ 8 4
        ♡ J 10 7 5 4               ♡ A 9 6 2
        ◇ A K 10      W       E    ◇ 9 4
        ♣ A 8 6              S     ♣ Q 7 4 3 2
                    ♠ A Q J 9 5 3
                    ♡ K
                    ◇ 8 7 3 2
                    ♣ 10 5
```

In this layout, after West takes his ace and king of diamonds, he should cash his club ace before giving East his ruff. This will keep East from underleading his ace of hearts.

In the actual quiz it is important to note the play of the heart ten. This card denied the queen and persuaded North to take his ace rather than try a greedy jack. This is a reasonably common situation when the defense is cashing out its winners.

Note also North's return of the club eight. This high spot implied lack of a high card in the suit. On this hand it was of no consequence because all the club honors were in view.

9

♠ Q 9
♡ Q 9 8 3 2
◇ A J 5
♣ A J 3

Vul vs not I open ONE HEART in first chair. LHO overcalls ONE SPADE and when partner passes, RHO raises to TWO SPADES. This hand was slightly better than a minimum when it started but it has gotten worse. I pass and two spades becomes the final contract.

Dealer: South
Vul: North-South

SOUTH	WEST	NORTH	EAST
1 ♡	1 ♠	Pass	2 ♠
Pass	Pass	Pass	

Partner starts with the ace of hearts.

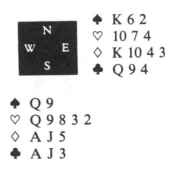

♠ K 6 2
♡ 10 7 4
◇ K 10 4 3
♣ Q 9 4

♠ Q 9
♡ Q 9 8 3 2
◇ A J 5
♣ A J 3

Is this a good lead for us?

Not particularly. Partner probably has a doubleton heart and unless it is the ace-jack we aren't going to get another heart trick. My heart bid appears to have gotten partner off to a bad lead. Without it we might have taken two heart tricks. Now, if declarer has KJx, as expected, we will get just one.

What should I play? Should I ask for a club or a diamond? While it's possible that either a club or a diamond switch would be right, it is most unlikely that it is imperative for partner to shift. Further, I have no idea which minor is correct, and there is no way I can direct a shift, even if I knew what I wanted.

Playing the heart queen might ask for a diamond switch but that would lose whenever partner had the AJ alone in hearts. The nine and eight of hearts would be encouraging and the three and two discouraging. Nothing I play could be construed as asking for a club shift.

Since I don't like hearts, and since I can't give a suit preference, should I just play the two and let partner work it out?

The one thing I'm not going to do is play the two. I have no idea that either minor is right and suspect that either one could be terrible. Why give partner a headache when he can't possibly come up with the right answer. I'm going to play the nine of hearts and ask for more hearts. True, we will gain nothing by this, but we will lose nothing either.

Partner continues with the heart five to declarer's jack.

Declarer proceeds to draw trumps, picking up my queen in the process and eventually loses two diamonds and a club. We are minus one forty.

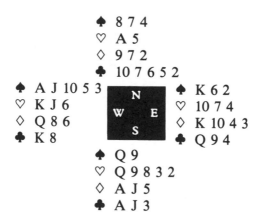

```
              ♠ 8 7 4
              ♡ A 5
              ◇ 9 7 2
              ♣ 10 7 6 5 2
♠ A J 10 5 3      N        ♠ K 6 2
♡ K J 6                    ♡ 10 7 4
◇ Q 8 6     W       E      ◇ K 10 4 3
♣ K 8             S        ♣ Q 9 4
              ♠ Q 9
              ♡ Q 9 8 3 2
              ◇ A J 5
              ♣ A J 3
```

A look at the entire hand shows that it was necessary to have partner continue hearts. A switch to either minor would have cost one trick.

The principle here is a simple one. Even though partner's lead was ineffective, it was best to encourage because the alternatives were worse.

FURTHER ANALYSIS

This principle can be carried even further. After ONE HEART by you and a direct THREE NOTRUMP by LHO, partner leads the heart king.

♠ Q 7 6
♡ J 6 4
◇ J 8 7 5
♣ Q 3 2

♠ 8 4 2
♡ A 10 8 5 3
◇ A K Q 10
♣ 7

If you could get partner to lead a diamond, you could beat this hand at least two. But since partner won't know what to switch to if you play the three, encourage a heart continuation and satisfy yourself with down one.

For the curious, declarer's hand was:

♠ A K
♡ Q 9 2
◇ 9 4
♣ A K J 10 6 4

♠ 10 9 2
♡ J 7 5
◇ K 5
♣ A Q J 5 4

When RHO opens ONE NOTRUMP, showing fifteen to seventeen, I pass. LHO tries TWO CLUBS, Stayman, and RHO denies a major suit with TWO DIAMONDS. LHO bids TWO NOTRUMP and RHO declines the invitation.

Dealer: East
Vul: None

EAST	SOUTH	WEST	NORTH
1 NT	Pass	2 ♣	Pass
2 ◇	Pass	2 NT	Pass
Pass	Pass		

On lead against two notrump, I inquire if this sequence by responder shows a major suit. I am told it does.

Rightly or wrongly I start with the ten of spades. If my clubs weren't so good I would lead them, but as it is, they may run without my having to concede a trick. This could work out poorly if the king appears in dummy. I expect this to happen less than thirty percent of the time. Also, partner may not get in.

Against this the opponents don't have too much. Two notrump is seldom played when there is any chance for game. Someone or other takes the push. If it's going to be close I don't want to give away a trick needlessly. So, with mild misgivings, I lead the spade ten and the good news is that dummy does not have the king of clubs.

♠ A 5
♡ K 8 6 3
◇ Q 10 8 4
♣ 9 7 6

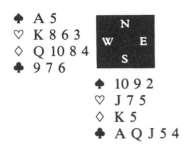

♠ 10 9 2
♡ J 7 5
◇ K 5
♣ A Q J 5 4

The bad news is that dummy has a maximum. Some might even have gone to game rather than invite.

My spade lead is ducked in dummy to partner's queen and declarer's king. This marks declarer with KJ or KJx. He follows with the diamond ace.

What are the chances for the defense?

It doesn't look too promising. Declarer probably has four diamonds, if not five, and this will give him three tricks in diamonds at least, two in hearts and probably three in spades.

Can partner have the king of clubs?

I can count on declarer for fifteen points, guaranteed by his opening bid. Dummy has nine, so these plus my eleven mean partner can have a maximum of five. I have seen the queen of spades and from the way declarer is playing the diamonds I expect partner to have the jack. This is three of partner's potential five. There's no room for the club king.

What can the defense do?

Since I am playing partner for the jack of diamonds and no king of clubs, I am going to dump the king of diamonds under the ace.

Declarer continues a diamond to dummy's queen and partner's nine. The third diamond goes to partner's jack. I choose to discard the nine of spades although there is not much to this. I did not throw the king of diamonds without a purpose and a club return is surely what I had in mind. Now it remains to be seen whether partner has the 10x of clubs or three small and whether or not he will lead one.

Partner leads the ten, a good sign, and when declarer ducks, partner continues the suit. This suffices for one down.

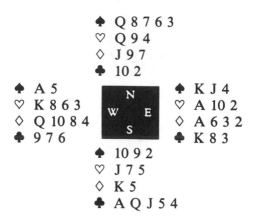

```
                    ♠ Q 8 7 6 3
                    ♡ Q 9 4
                    ◊ J 9 7
                    ♣ 10 2
  ♠ A 5                              ♠ K J 4
  ♡ K 8 6 3            N             ♡ A 10 2
  ◊ Q 10 8 4       W       E         ◊ A 6 3 2
  ♣ 9 7 6              S             ♣ K 8 3
                    ♠ 10 9 2
                    ♡ J 7 5
                    ◊ K 5
                    ♣ A Q J 5 4
```

It is evident that declarer suspected I had a doubleton diamond. It would be a strange play to continue the suit if he thought North had J97x. My play of the king apparently was not exactly in tempo.

FURTHER ANALYSIS

Declarer must have known South had a good club holding to account for the extreme effort to get North on lead. Declarer was probably hoping South had only four clubs. Otherwise, he could have ducked a heart into my hand and ended up with three spades, three hearts and two diamonds.

On some hands, it might be sound play for South to dump the king of diamonds, not as an effort to get North in, but to convince declarer that the suit had no future. For this to work the defender must play his king with no apparent thought.

11

♠ A Q J 7 2
♡ A 10 3
◇ 9 4 3
♣ 4 3

No one is vul and in third chair I open an unexceptional ONE SPADE. LHO seems a little agitated and emerges with FOUR CLUBS. No one has anything further to say and partner leads the eight of spades.

Dealer: North
Vul: None

NORTH	EAST	SOUTH	WEST
Pass	Pass	1 ♠	4 ♣
Pass	Pass	Pass	

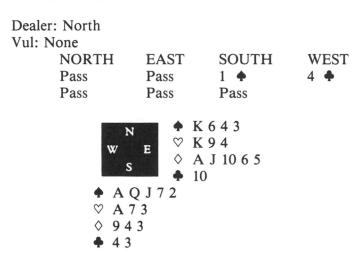

♠ K 6 4 3
♡ K 9 4
◇ A J 10 6 5
♣ 10

♠ A Q J 7 2
♡ A 7 3
◇ 9 4 3
♣ 4 3

Dummy plays low and my jack wins. Declarer drops the nine. The lead marks declarer with the ten of spades so I can be sure of at least a second spade trick. I'm also sure the heart ace will cash.

Why?

If partner had the missing seven hearts he would likely have preempted three hearts. Therefore he doesn't have them.

How to continue?

There are a number of possibilities. I can exit immediately with a club and hope we have club trick coming, or perhaps two hearts, or perhaps a diamond. However I do not expect partner to have a diamond trick. With the KQ(xxx) he might have led one. Also, if I exit a club, declarer may be able to win and take a discard on the diamonds. It would be embarrassing to end up taking a club trick and still not beat them.

Since partner may have a singleton spade I'm going to cash the ace. Declarer and partner both follow.

Should I lead another spade? Why?

I intend to do this eventually but first I cash the ace of hearts. I do this before leading the spade because declarer could discard his heart loser on the spade lead while partner scores his ruff.

The heart ace wins and when I switch back to spades partner leans back a bit and it's clear that this has been successful.

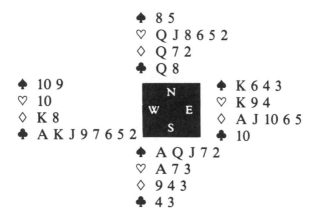

```
                    ♠ 8 5
                    ♡ Q J 8 6 5 2
                    ◇ Q 7 2
                    ♣ Q 8
    ♠ 10 9                          ♠ K 6 4 3
    ♡ 10               N            ♡ K 9 4
    ◇ K 8        W          E       ◇ A J 10 6 5
    ♣ A K J 9 7 6 5 2     S         ♣ 10
                    ♠ A Q J 7 2
                    ♡ A 7 3
                    ◇ 9 4 3
                    ♣ 4 3
```

This defense will work whenever partner has Jxx or Qx of clubs. Every now and then it will be the only defense to hold declarer to four.

As against this it is possible that this is the only defense to allow them to make four clubs. For instance, partner could have both diamond honors.

FURTHER ANALYSIS

It is the nature of defense that you often have to reason from various clues as opposed to concrete facts. Some of the time your clues are reasonably strong as they were on this hand. Some of the time they are extremely awkward to judge and you may decide to ignore them completely and try a different tack.

Perhaps you can try a swindle rather than look for a legitimate defense. Or you may decide declarer hasn't got his bid or has made a mistake.

Defense is not an exact science.

12

♠ A 7 2
♡ A K 9 4 2
◇ Q 10 4
♣ 10 6

Vul vs not I open ONE HEART in second seat. LHO DOUBLES and partner skips to THREE HEARTS. RHO DOUBLES and LHO alerts this as being a responsive double. I pass and LHO takes it out to THREE SPADES. Opposite partner's preemptive raise I have a rather dull hand so when partner and RHO pass I do so as well.

Dealer: East
Vul: North-South

EAST	SOUTH	WEST	NORTH
Pass	1 ♡	Double	3 ♡
Double*	Pass	3 ♠	Pass
Pass	Pass		

*responsive

Partner leads the jack of hearts.

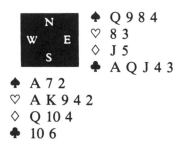

♠ Q 9 8 4
♡ 8 3
◇ J 5
♣ A Q J 4 3

♠ A 7 2
♡ A K 9 4 2
◇ Q 10 4
♣ 10 6

I win the heart king and cash the ace as declarer drops the queen. The spade ace will be our third trick so we will either need two diamonds or we will have to score a second spade trick.

Should I lead a trump?

This is dangerous as partner could have the doubleton jack. A trump shift would kill this potential trick.

Should I lead a diamond?

This is a distinct possibility. If partner has the king we will set up a trick and can hope for a second spade. If partner has the ace we will get a trick immediately and if declarer errs by putting up the king we beat them immediately.

If partner has the ace of diamonds must I lead a diamond now? Can declarer discard his diamonds if given the chance?

No. Declarer most likely has only four spades, or else he would have overcalled, two hearts which we have seen, and consequently seven cards in the minors.

What does this mean?

No matter what declarer's minor suit distribution is, he will not be able to get rid of his diamond losers. For example, if he has four diamonds and three clubs he will be able to discard two diamonds but will be left with two. Therefore, if partner has the ace of diamonds declarer will have to lose two diamonds at the end of the hand. Therefore a diamond lead now cannot gain and may lose.

If partner has the king of diamonds that will keep too. There is no reason to lead a diamond now.

Is this one hundred percent?

No, if declarer has five spades, then he will have only six minor suit cards. Also, if declarer happens to have a third heart, this plan will misfire.

Is either of these things possible?

Declarer might have five spades, but it is unlikely. For him to have three hearts is almost impossible. It would require partner to have jump raised on three card support and declarer to have made a very unusual false card.

What is the right play after winning the two top hearts?

Since both spades and diamonds are dangerous, and because a heart would give a sluff-ruff, the best play is the 10 of clubs. Declarer wins with dummy's jack and attacks spades. After winning the ace, I can see no reason to change my thinking so I exit with another club. Declarer wins this, draws trump and runs the clubs. Eventually, he leads a diamond to his king and partner produces the ace. My queen is the setting trick.

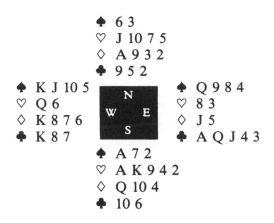

♠ 6 3
♡ J 10 7 5
◇ A 9 3 2
♣ 9 5 2

♠ K J 10 5   ♠ Q 9 8 4
♡ Q 6   ♡ 8 3
◇ K 8 7 6   ◇ J 5
♣ K 8 7   ♣ A Q J 4 3

♠ A 7 2
♡ A K 9 4 2
◇ Q 10 4
♣ 10 6

FURTHER ANALYSIS

As a defender you will often have to decide whether or not to open up a suit. Frequently you can answer this question by counting declarer's tricks. If you can see that declarer will ultimately have to play a suit himself, as on this hand, you should wait and let him do so rather than attack it yourself.

Change the bidding and hand slightly:

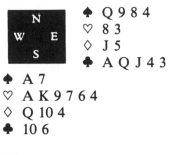

♠ Q 9 8 4
♡ 8 3
◇ J 5
♣ A Q J 4 3

♠ A 7
♡ A K 9 7 6 4
◇ Q 10 4
♣ 10 6

WEST	NORTH	EAST	SOUTH
1 ♠*	Pass	2 ♣	2 ♡
3 ♣	Pass	3 ♠	Pass
4 ♠	Pass	Pass	Pass

*Five card majors

Partner leads the heart two and you cash two hearts, declarer playing the queen and ten, partner following suit. This time it's right to lead a diamond. If partner has nothing in diamonds nothing is lost. But if partner has the king it is necessary to get it before declarer can take his ten tricks in the form of four spades, one diamond and five clubs. Finally if partner has the diamond ace you will lose nothing by leading a diamond. Declarer will have a maximum of one diamond to lose if you wait, and may misguess and put up the king, losing two tricks in the suit.

The important difference between the two hands is the number of minor suit cards held by declarer. In the first hand he held seven minor suit cards, so that, even after running dummy's five clubs, he would still be left with two diamonds. In the second, he held only six minor suit cards at most. Therefore, the run of the clubs would leave him with only one diamond. This made it necessary for the defense to attack diamonds before the clubs could be run to be sure of getting its diamond tricks. Note the important differences between the two versions of this hand. They are worth reviewing.

13

♠ Q 5 4
♡ J 10 8
◇ A 10 5
♣ Q 10 9 7

Vul vs not, I hear ONE SPADE from LHO and RHO responds ONE NOTRUMP. I have nothing to say when LHO's TWO SPADES is passed around, I pass again.

Dealer: West
Vul: North-South

WEST	NORTH	EAST	SOUTH
1 ♠	Pass	1 NT	Pass
2 ♠	Pass	Pass	Pass

Partner's opening lead is the diamond two.

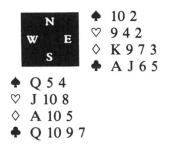

♠ 10 2
♡ 9 4 2
◇ K 9 7 3
♣ A J 6 5

♠ Q 5 4
♡ J 10 8
◇ A 10 5
♣ Q 10 9 7

Dummy plays the seven and I have to decide what to play to this trick, and, if I win, what to do next.

First, should I play the ten?

Since partner would lead the queen from queen-jack, I can place declarer with one of these cards. Also, partner's lead shows either three or four diamonds so declarer has at least two. I suppose it's possible that the lead is a singleton, but the bidding makes that unlikely. I'm defending on the premise that partner has three or more diamonds.

Given the above, I'm not going to play the ten because declarer would win it with whichever honor he has and could later finesse the nine to establish a second trick.

The five would be a far better play than the ten because it wouldn't give declarer a second trick if he has the jack.

If I win the trick how should I continue?

The obvious shift is to a heart but I'm going to examine a club shift as well. Neither a spade nor a diamond play has any appeal.

Leading a heart is both aggressive and safe so there will have to be a lot to be said for a club shift before I make that play.

Why might a club play be necessary?

If partner has the king of clubs, a club play will be effective defense because it will remove declarer's entry to dummy before he can untangle his diamond winners. If declarer has Qx of diamonds, he won't be able to cash the queen and king separately, and if he has Jx of diamonds, he won't be able to establish the nine and then use it.

Does partner have the king of clubs?

This is not certain, but there is a reasonable chance. Partner does not have the king-queen or the ace-king of hearts or he would have led one instead of this nebulous diamond. Declarer therefore has at least the heart king and could easily have better. Declarer also has six or seven spades which may be as good as the AKJ. He also has a diamond honor. All in all, it looks like partner is quite likely to hold the club king. Also, if declarer has the Kx of clubs exactly, a club lead will not give an extra trick because declarer won't be able to untangle both his club suit and his diamond suit. True the club lead will cost when declarer has the club king and only the heart king. In this case we could take three fast heart tricks.

Considering all of this I do shift to a club. Since I want partner to play the king if he has it, I lead the seven rather than the ten. Declarer follows with the eight and partner produces the king. Dummy wins the ace. Declarer now plays off three rounds of spades to my queen, partner having J7 originally.

Finally comes the heart shift. My heart jack goes to declarer's king and partner's ace. Partner returns a small heart and my eight wins. I continue with the heart ten and partner overtakes with the queen as declarer follows. When partner shifts to a club declarer ducks in dummy and ruffs my ten. Two more rounds of spades are produced but nothing good happens for declarer and we score one more diamond.

The entire hand turns out to be a bit of an embarrassment.

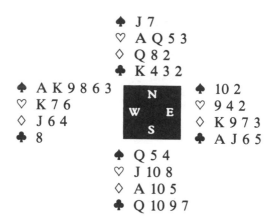

```
              ♠ J 7
              ♡ A Q 5 3
              ◇ Q 8 2
              ♣ K 4 3 2
♠ A K 9 8 6 3                 ♠ 10 2
♡ K 7 6          N            ♡ 9 4 2
◇ J 6 4      W       E        ◇ K 9 7 3
♣ 8              S            ♣ A J 6 5
              ♠ Q 5 4
              ♡ J 10 8
              ◇ A 10 5
              ♣ Q 10 9 7
```

Almost any defense would have worked except a diamond return or the ten of diamonds at trick one.

Nonetheless, the defensive considerations were sound. Declarer could have had one of a number of other hands such as these:

```
        A                B                C
♠ A K 9 8 6 3     ♠ A J 8 7 6 3     ♠ A J 8 7 6 3
♡ K Q 7           ♡ A K 6           ♡ A Q 6
◇ Q 6             ◇ J 6             ◇ J 6
♣ 8 3             ♣ 8 2             ♣ 8 2
```

Note that on the first of these hands the play of the diamond five at trick one would not work. Declarer would play the high trumps and then establish a second diamond trick. On the next two hands the five would not cost a trick. In all cases the best defense is the diamond ace followed by a club. Note that in the second and third examples declarer would win a heart shift and lead the diamond jack. Partner would have to cover with the queen and declarer would be able to ruff the next diamond, felling your ten.

FURTHER ANALYSIS

On example hand A, if you shift to a heart the defense can survive if partner shifts to a club rather than clearing the hearts. But that would be difficult for him to find.

Note that on the actual hand partner, when he won the heart ace, did not thoughtlessly bang down the heart queen. This would have endplayed you nicely and your thoughtful defense would have been for naught.

I note that partner chose to lead from Q82 of diamonds rather than K432 of clubs. Curious, but maybe he was influenced by the eight of diamonds. In any event, there is not much to choose from.

14

♠ J 8 3
♡ 6 5 2
◇ 8 7 6 4
♣ 9 6 5

Playing against a pair I know to be quite unsound with both sides vulnerable, my partner passes. RHO opens ONE SPADE and LHO jumps to TWO NOTRUMP. When RHO rebids THREE SPADES LHO continues with an emphatic THREE NOTRUMP.

Dealer: North
Vul: Both

NORTH	EAST	SOUTH	WEST
Pass	1 ♠	Pass	2 NT
Pass	3 ♠	Pass	3 NT
Pass	Pass	Pass	

Partner leads the queen of hearts and a mildly surprising dummy appears. I guess this pair plays that three notrump ends all auctions.

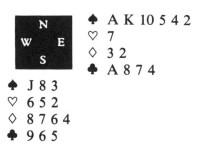

♠ A K 10 5 4 2
♡ 7
◇ 3 2
♣ A 8 7 4

♠ J 8 3
♡ 6 5 2
◇ 8 7 6 4
♣ 9 6 5

The lead goes to declarer's king as I follow with the two. LHO follows with the nine of diamonds which wins, partner playing the five and I the eight. Next comes the ten of diamonds to partner's ace and my four.

Partner continues with the heart nine and this is permitted to win.

What's going on?

At this point declarer is known to have five diamonds KQJ109, the ace and king of hearts and one or two small spades plus something in clubs.

Why can't declarer have the queen of spades or three small?

Because he would win the heart and attempt to run the spades. Also declarer might have bid differently, although against this particular LHO I am not anxious to draw conclusions from the bidding.

Is it possible that I have misread either the hearts or the diamonds?

The diamonds are clear cut as partner would not false card. The hearts could be AQJ109(x) in partner's hand rather than AK in declarer's, but if this is the case, partner will cash out the suit.

Partner leads the heart ten and declarer finally takes this. In the meantime dummy has discarded one spade and one club.

When declarer cashes the diamond king partner discards the heart three. This confirms nine tricks for declarer and we are merely exercising for some overtricks.

What can you do with this hand to contribute to the defense?

Assuming that partner has the queen of spades, a fairly safe assumption even given this particular declarer, you can control the spade suit. If partner has Qx of spades he won't have any worries about spades. Whatever happens will happen. But if he has Qxx he may not know he can afford a spade discard. From his point of view declarer ought to have a doubleton spade so he can't afford to throw one. Instead he will probably throw clubs.

Can you tell partner that spades are safe to discard?

Yes, on this diamond trick I can follow with the seven. Since I have already given count, partner will understand this as suit preference for spades. Partner has also seen declarer's bidding before and will draw the correct inference.

Declarer takes his winners but ultimately I score the spade jack. We have held declarer to ten tricks.

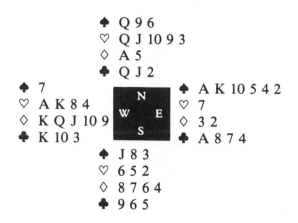

♠ Q 9 6
♡ Q J 10 9 3
◇ A 5
♣ Q J 2

♠ 7
♡ A K 8 4
◇ K Q J 10 9
♣ K 10 3

♠ A K 10 5 4 2
♡ 7
◇ 3 2
♣ A 8 7 4

♠ J 8 3
♡ 6 5 2
◇ 8 7 6 4
♣ 9 6 5

FURTHER ANALYSIS

Declarer played the diamond suit in a silly fashion. The play of the king at trick two would have hidden his actual holding from the defenders and made it more difficult for them to communicate.

Note that South had to consider the unsoundness of his opponents. If South never considered that West might have a stiff spade, it might not occur to him to give partner any help on defense. Note that a club discard by North would prove fatal.

If declarer, on the run of his red suits, discards small spades from dummy, South must hold his 965 of clubs. As long as dummy holds three clubs, so too must South.

15

♠ J 8 7
♡ Q 5
◇ Q 9 2
♣ A K J 9 5

Vul vs not, RHO opens ONE SPADE. As much as I like to mix it up, this hand does not have the qualifications. It has bad shape, a poor spade holding, and too many soft values. I pass. LHO responds TWO HEARTS. When opener rebids TWO SPADES, his partner raises to FOUR SPADES. I have no reason to doubt they can make this and pass it out.

Dealer: East
Vul: East-West

EAST	SOUTH	WEST	NORTH
1 ♠	Pass	2 ♡	Pass
2 ♠	Pass	4 ♠	Pass
Pass	Pass		

The king of clubs looks like the normal lead and I make it.

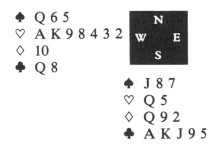

♠ Q 6 5
♡ A K 9 8 4 3 2
◇ 10
♣ Q 8

♠ J 8 7
♡ Q 5
◇ Q 9 2
♣ A K J 9 5

The first two tricks are easy as I cash two club tricks, partner playing the two-six and declarer the three-four.

At trick three I have my first real decision of the hand. I'm not leading a trump as this could blow the setting trick by removing any guess declarer has in the spade suit. And I'm not leading a heart. A passive defense could be best but I think I can make a strong case for either a diamond or a further club.

On this particular hand, it is important whether the game is IMP's or matchpoints, While in general this book is aimed at fundamentals, an occasional hand creeps in where the form of scoring matters. This is one of them.

At matchpoints, for instance, you might judge it necessary to switch to a diamond in order to hold declarer to four should partner hold the ace of diamonds.

Let us assume the scoring is IMP's or, if you prefer, rubber bridge, and your sole objective is to beat four spades.

Can it be done?

Perhaps.

The first thing to do is determine if it can be beaten on brute strength; i.e. How much can partner contribute?

Given the values in my hand and in dummy, it is reasonable that partner can have the ace or king of spades or the ace or king of diamonds. It is unreasonable that partner have more than one of these cards.

Therefore, leading a diamond will be a hopeless defense. If partner has the ace or king, then declarer will have the high spades and will simply set up the hearts and draw trumps ending in dummy. If declarer is void in hearts, he may have trouble, but, if so, he will have trouble no matter what he has.

Is it possible that partner's two-six of clubs was a suit preference for diamonds?

Absolutely not. Partner has done nothing unusual. He was just following suit.

What's left is a club.

Why a club?

Leading the jack of clubs will remove one of dummy's trumps. This will preclude declarer's setting up the heart suit unless it is already good (if declarer has two or three hearts). Since declarer is likely to have a singleton heart, a club continuation holds substantial promise.

Is it possible that declarer has two clubs and will get a sluff-ruff on the third round of clubs.?

Yes. This is possible. Partner was not able to distinguish between three and four clubs.

Can a sluff-ruff give away the contract?

Unlikely. The only likely loss would be a diamond trick and if partner has the diamond ace then the contract was probably cold.

I finally lead the club jack and declarer spends quite a bit of time on his play. It feels like we have some chances. Declarer probably has a five card spade suit because with six he would have various easy routes to ten tricks. Eventually declarer pitches a small heart from dummy. When partner and declarer follow to the club I am still on play.

What now?

From declarer's choice of plays it is clear that he has the ace of diamonds and, most likely, both spade honors as well. There is still an answer to this though and if partner can cooperate, it will produce a sure set.

At trick four I continue with yet another club and partner is there with the ten of spades. Declarer overruffs but now has a trump loser. The result is one down.

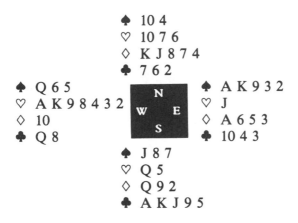

```
                    ♠ 10 4
                    ♡ 10 7 6
                    ◊ K J 8 7 4
                    ♣ 7 6 2
♠ Q 6 5                          ♠ A K 9 3 2
♡ A K 9 8 4 3 2       N          ♡ J
◊ 10              W       E      ◊ A 6 5 3
♣ Q 8                S           ♣ 10 4 3
                    ♠ J 8 7
                    ♡ Q 5
                    ◊ Q 9 2
                    ♣ A K J 9 5
```

Note the difference between matchpoints and IMP's. The club continuation could easily cost an overtrick and turn an average board into a zero.

FURTHER ANALYSIS

Declarer did well not to ruff the third club, but he erred psychologically. If he had pitched the diamond ten from dummy at trick three instead of a heart, it would have created the possibility that he was missing the ace of diamonds. The best defense would then be unclear. Should South play North for the ace of diamonds and try to tap dummy with a diamond lead or should South play North for the spade ten and go for an uppercut?

16

♠ A K 9 8 3
♡ 6 3
◇ 9 7 6
♣ A Q 2

In first chair, with no one vulnerable, I open this unexceptional hand with ONE SPADE. Both LHO and partner pass and RHO reopens with a DOUBLE. I can't imagine any excuse for bidding so I pass. LHO bids TWO CLUBS and it's clear from his tone that he doesn't like it. My partner now discovers he has a few odds and ends and comes back in with TWO SPADES. Any thoughts that we might buy this hand are quickly squelched as RHO calls a confident FOUR HEARTS. I can easily visualize seven or eight losers opposite a hand that could not raise the first time, so I pass. Four hearts becomes the final contract and I lead the spade king.

Dealer: South
Vul: None

SOUTH	WEST	NORTH	EAST
1 ♠	Pass	Pass	Double
Pass	2 ♣	2 ♠	4 ♡
Pass	Pass	Pass	

```
              ♠ J 7
              ♡ Q 10 5           N
              ◇ 10 8 4 2     W        E
              ♣ J 8 4 3           S
                         ♠ A K 9 8 3
                         ♡ 6 3
                         ◇ 9 7 6
                         ♣ A Q 2
```

Dummy is complaining that he has only four points, but on this sequence that looks like a pretty good hand to me.

On my king of spades dummy plays the seven, partner the ten and declarer the six.

What does the ten of spades mean?

Since partner voluntarily raised spades I don't think he has a doubleton. I think he has the queen and is telling me I can get him in with it.

What does this suggest?

It looks like our best chance to beat four hearts is to take two spades and two clubs. The way to do this is to underlead the spade ace and have partner return a club.

Is there any danger that partner will return a diamond rather than a club? Is it possible that it doesn't matter what he returns?

There is a strong chance that partner, if left to his own devices, will return a diamond and this could easily cost the contract. To thwart this, I lead the spade three at trick two. Partner takes his queen and, interpreting the spade three correctly, returns the club five. Declarer plays the six and I win the queen and ace of clubs. They are one down.

♠ Q 10 5 2
♡ 7 4
◇ J 5 3
♣ 10 9 7 5

♠ J 7   ♠ 6 4
♡ Q 10 5   ♡ A K J 9 8 2
◇ 10 8 4 2   ◇ A K Q
♣ J 8 4 3   ♣ K 6

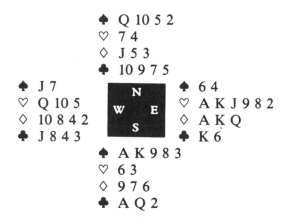

♠ A K 9 8 3
♡ 6 3
◇ 9 7 6
♣ A Q 2

On this hand the defense could afford no errors. If South failed to underlead the ace of spades, or if North returned a diamond, declarer could break the diamonds 3-3 and score dummy's ten of diamonds for his tenth trick.

FURTHER ANALYSIS

When partner returned the five of clubs it would not have helped declarer to falsecard with the king. If the king were singleton it would mean that partner had returned the club five from 109765. That would be impossible.

But if the six and five of clubs were reversed, so that declarer had the K5, and partner returned the six, a falsecard of the king would be credible.

Without suit preference partner would have had to guess whether declarer had something like:

♠ xx
♡ AKxxxxx
◇ Kx
♣ AK

Now if partner returned a club declarer could set up the jack of clubs for a diamond discard. On this layout a diamond switch is necessary. The solution of course is provided by the spade spot led to North's queen at trick two.

17

♠ 10 4 3
♡ Q 8 4
◇ K 5 4 2
♣ J 4 2

We are not vul vs vul, LHO opens ONE DIAMOND, and my partner DOUBLES. RHO bids ONE HEART which I ascertain is forcing. I am a strong believer in competing when partner makes a takeout double and if I had four spades I would certainly bid them. My only option here is to bid one notrump and I'm not quite strong enough for that. If I had one more point plus, say, the ten of diamonds, I would chance it.

I pass and LHO's TWO DIAMOND rebid is passed out.

Dealer: West
Vul: East-West

WEST	NORTH	EAST	SOUTH
1 ◇	Double	1 ♡	Pass
2 ◇	Pass	Pass	Pass

Partner leads the king of hearts.

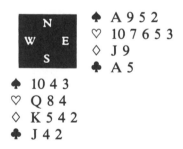

♠ A 9 5 2
♡ 10 7 6 5 3
◇ J 9
♣ A 5

♠ 10 4 3
♡ Q 8 4
◇ K 5 4 2
♣ J 4 2

Since I don't want a shift I encourage with the eight, declarer following with the two. Partner continues with the heart ace which declarer ruffs. Declarer plays a club to the ace, a club to his king and ruffs a club in dummy with the nine. Partner has played the 6, 7, 8 in clubs so I presume he has five of them.

Dummy leads the jack of diamonds. I duck and declarer overtakes with the queen. Next comes the ace and ten of diamonds
to my king. Partner had one diamond and has discarded two
clubs.

We have arrived at this position:

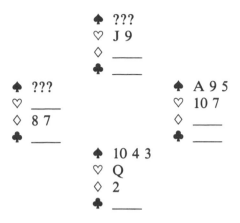

What should I play? More important, why?

It is easy to construct combinations where a spade lead would
be disastrous. If declarer has QJx

or KJx

or J8x

then a spade lead will cost a trick.

The heart queen leads to a different sort of problem. As the
hand stands now both partner and I have heart control. But if I
lead the heart queen declarer will ruff and when he draws the
last trump partner may find it impossible to protect both spades
and hearts.

I can exit with a diamond. Now partner will not feel any pressure because he can discard his hearts. Whatever will happen in
spades will happen and declarer will not have the advantage of
my breaking the suit for him.

I do choose the diamond and we hold declarer to ten tricks.

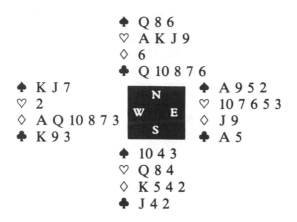

♠ Q 8 6
♡ A K J 9
◇ 6
♣ Q 10 8 7 6

♠ K J 7
♡ 2
◇ A Q 10 8 7 3
♣ K 9 3

♠ A 9 5 2
♡ 10 7 6 5 3
◇ J 9
♣ A 5

♠ 10 4 3
♡ Q 8 4
◇ K 5 4 2
♣ J 4 2

Declarer could have made eleven tricks in a number of ways. He could have ruffed hearts in his hand, scoring six trump tricks, two spades, two clubs and a ruff.

Or more elegant, but less certain, he could have ruffed a second heart in hand and then conceded a diamond to South. Now North would be squeezed.

FURTHER ANALYSIS

Note that North's double was made on a light hand and could easily have been made on less. For this reason responder should be less inclined to compete in notrump than in a suit. The takeout double is more indicative of shape than high card values.

18

♠ A 6 2
♡ K J 5 2
◇ A 9 4 2
♣ 9 7

Vul vs not, partner passes and RHO opens ONE SPADE.
Some would double with this hand but to me that borders on ir-
rational. I pass. LHO responds TWO DIAMONDS and RHO
rebids TWO HEARTS. It looks like bidding earlier would have
been a disaster. The auction continues with TWO SPADES by
LHO and FOUR SPADES by opener. I have a good hand but
not so good that I'm going to double.

Dealer: North
Vul: North-South

NORTH	EAST	SOUTH	WEST
Pass	1 ♠	Pass	2 ◇
Pass	2 ♡	Pass	2 ♠
Pass	4 ♠	Pass	Pass

Before leading I check their convention card. The sequence
chosen by responder was intended to show ten or eleven points
with spade support and some sort of diamond holding. In this
day of science one doesn't run into this approach too much any
more.

I have a choice of opening leads. I can lead a small trump or I
can lead the nine of clubs. Nothing else appeals. Having a good
holding in declarer's second suit I decide to lead the trump two,
but I don't feel strongly about it.

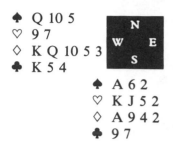

```
       ♠ Q 10 5
       ♡ 9 7
       ◇ K Q 10 5 3
       ♣ K 5 4

                  ♠ A 6 2
                  ♡ K J 5 2
                  ◇ A 9 4 2
                  ♣ 9 7
```

The play goes two, five, seven and declarer's nine. At trick two declarer leads the seven of diamonds and I have a common problem. Should I grab this? If so, what next? Or should I duck and hope we have four defensive tricks outside of diamonds?

First, what is declarer's shape? Does he have a stiff diamond?

At this stage it isn't really known. He probably is five-four in the majors. With five-five he might have rebid hearts. It is possible he is six-four. In all these cases it is highly probable he has a stiff diamond so it is useful to look at the problem from that perspective. If it looks like it will be impossible to beat four spades against a singleton diamond in RHO's hand then it will be necessary to make a different assumption.

Should I grab the diamond?

This is a common problem. Frequently solving it requires that you ask another question, i.e., if I take this trick can I see where the setting tricks will come from. In this case if you take the ace of diamonds you will need partner to have:

1. the ace and queen of clubs or
2. the ace of hearts.

Can partner have the club ace and queen? Unlikely, as that would leave declarer with something like:

```
       ♠ KJ9xx
       ♡ AQxxx
       ◇ x
       ♣ Jx
```

This does not look like a four spade bid.

Can partner have the heart ace? This is barely possible. Declarer might have:

58

♠ KJ9xx
♡ Qxxxx
◇ x
♣ AQ

although this is a bit thin.

All in all, it looks like taking the ace of diamonds is unlikely to be effective. I won't entirely reject it but first I want to see what will happen if I duck this trick. Hence the second question. Should I duck the diamond? Once again the answer can frequently be determined by asking another question, which is "If declarer sneaks by a singleton, and I lose my ace, where will the tricks come from to beat them?"

This time the answer is easy. If declarer wins the diamond king, he will still have numerous losers whenever he has something along these lines:

♠ KJ9xx	♠ KJxxxx	♠ KJxxx
♡ AQxxx	♡ AQxx	♡ AQxx
◇ x	◇ x	◇ x
♣ Qx	♣ Qx	♣ Axx

and he may still go down if he has:

♠ KJ9xx
♡ AQxx
◇ x
♣ AJ10

and misguesses clubs.

It seems far more practical to hope for partner to have the queen and jack of clubs or any ace at all rather than one of the hands he needs if I take the diamond.

Of particular note is that on any hand where they will go down if I take my ace, they will still go down if I refuse it.

In practice declarer won the diamond king and finessed the queen of hearts. Ace and another spade left declarer with a trumpless dummy. Declarer did manage to recover one trick by taking another heart finesse. This eventually allowed him two heart tricks when the ten dropped, but he finished one down.

The complete hand:

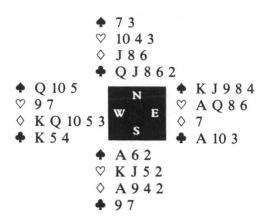

```
                ♠ 7 3
                ♡ 10 4 3
                ◇ J 8 6
                ♣ Q J 8 6 2
  ♠ Q 10 5                    ♠ K J 9 8 4
  ♡ 9 7          N            ♡ A Q 8 6
  ◇ K Q 10 5 3   W    E       ◇ 7
  ♣ K 5 4             S       ♣ A 10 3
                ♠ A 6 2
                ♡ K J 5 2
                ◇ A 9 4 2
                ♣ 9 7
```

FURTHER ANALYSIS

Deciding whether to take a trick when declarer leads a possible singleton towards dummy, or when declarer leads a singleton from dummy towards the closed hand, depends on many factors. As a rule, it is right to duck, but certainly there are times when you should not, e.g.

After:

RHO	YOU	LHO	PARTNER
1 ◇	Pass	1 ♠	Pass
2 ♣	Pass	3 ♣	Pass
5 ♣	Pass	Pass	Pass

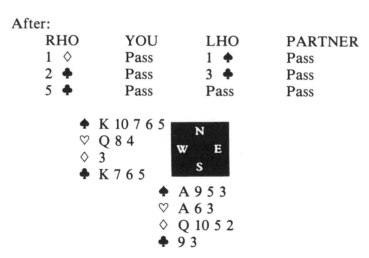

```
  ♠ K 10 7 6 5
  ♡ Q 8 4         N
  ◇ 3        W         E
  ♣ K 7 6 5       S
             ♠ A 9 5 3
             ♡ A 6 3
             ◇ Q 10 5 2
             ♣ 9 3
```

You lead, rightly or wrongly, a trump. Declarer wins and leads the spade four. Here it can easily be right to take the ace and switch to ace and a heart. The key is this: If you duck where will the setting trick come from?

19

♠ K J 8
♡ Q 10 8 5
♢ A J 9 3
♣ K 2

With no one vul, LHO opens ONE DIAMOND and RHO bids ONE HEART. With the opponents bidding both of my suits, I have nothing to say. LHO rebids ONE NOTRUMP and this is raised to THREE NO TRUMP. A case can be made for doubling, but I don't feel a heart lead is absolutely necessary. Anything partner leads will be fine. A spade or a club could be best and I don't want to talk partner out of his chosen lead. Partner chooses spades and leads the four.

Dealer: West
Vul: None

WEST	NORTH	EAST	SOUTH
1 ◇	Pass	1 ♡	Pass
1 NT	Pass	3 NT	Pass
Pass	Pass	Pass	

♠ A 3
♡ A K J 6
♢ 8 6 4
♣ 10 8 6 3

♠ K J 8
♡ Q 10 8 5
♢ A J 9 3
♣ K 2

Our style is to lead fourth best and we tend not to lead low unless we have something in the suit. From 87542 we would lead the eight or the seven.

With this in mind, how should the defense go? What are the crucial factors?

First, how do the spades divide?

From the auction it is probable that declarer does not have four spades, else he might have rebid one spade rather than one notrump. Weak notrumpers frequently rebid one notrump with all or most balanced 15-18 point hands and then use various conventions to find their fits. For such players, a one notrump rebid does not deny four spades.

Against the current opponents I would not expect to find declarer with four spades.

Partner's lead could could be from a five or six card suit, but the three in dummy means partner can have only one card smaller than the four, i.e. the two. Hence he is leading from exactly five spades.

What values can partner have?

Darn few. The opponents have around twenty five high card points, so with my fourteen, partner is left with one jack. If declarer has opened a twelve count, then partner could have a second jack, or perhaps a queen.

When dummy plays the three, I have to decide what to play to the first two tricks.

The obvious play is to take the king and return the jack. Now if partner has the five spades to the queen I am hoping for, they will be at least one down.

What if partner doesn't have the queen of spades?

Declarer will win the third round of spades and will probably be able to take nine tricks. There will be some nervous moments for him, but since partner doesn't have an entry declarer will eventually suceed.

Can I cater to declarer's having the queen of spades?

Yes. At trick one, I can play the jack of spades. If partner has the queen of spades, my jack will win and I will continue with the king. The position will be exactly as if I had won the king and returned the jack.

However, if declarer has the queen, as I suspect, he will win it, barring double dummy insight and I can later return the king to dummy's ace. If I get in again I will have a third spade to return and I will need to find partner with only the ten of spades.

Putting this into practice I play the jack and declarer takes his queen. Since the lead and auction mark him with three spades I am not concerned that I have given him an extra trick. Declarer continues with the diamond king to my ace. Now I play the king of spades. Declarer wins in dummy and finesses the ten of diamonds. Partner shows out as declarer evidences mixed emotions. For a few seconds when my partner did not produce the jack declarer was happy, but as partner contemplated his discard, declarer came to realize that diamonds were four-one.

Partner finally throws the club five. Declarer now tries the heart finesse. When this loses we cash out the spade suit for down one.

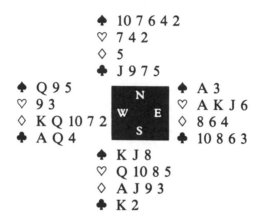

                    ♠ 10 7 6 4 2
                    ♡ 7 4 2
                    ◇ 5
                    ♣ J 9 7 5
    ♠ Q 9 5   ♠ A 3
    ♡ 9 3   N   ♡ A K J 6
    ◇ K Q 10 7 2   W   E   ◇ 8 6 4
    ♣ A Q 4   S   ♣ 10 8 6 3
                    ♠ K J 8
                    ♡ Q 10 8 5
                    ◇ A J 9 3
                    ♣ K 2

FURTHER ANALYSIS

If my partner had slightly different spade spots he might have been able to signal the quality of his suit, i.e.

                    A 9
    10 8 6 3 2   K J 7
                    Q 5 4

If the play went as discussed, spade three to the nine, jack and queen. Then later the king to the ace. Partner could play the ten to show the suit was now solid.

If the suit were changed slightly again

$$A\ 9$$
$$8\ 7\ 5\ 3\ 2 \qquad\qquad K\ J\ 6$$
$$Q\ 10\ 4$$

If West had led the three originally (not my choice) to the nine, jack and queen, and the play continued so that partner later returned the king, West would play the eight. This would deny the ten and would inform East of the spade position. It would advise East to look for an effective defense elsewhere.

20

♠ 6 5
♡ A 10 8 2
◇ J 10 8 7
♣ Q J 6

Not vul vs vul, I am in fourth seat. There are two passes and my RHO opens ONE SPADE. I pass and LHO raises to THREE SPADES. Everyone passes quickly and three spades becomes the final contract.

Dealer: West
Vul: East-West

WEST	NORTH	EAST	SOUTH
Pass	Pass	1 ♠	Pass
3 ♠	Pass	Pass	Pass
Pass			

Trumps could easily be the best lead but, perhaps swayed by the diamond seven, I lead the diamond jack.

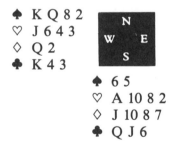

♠ K Q 8 2
♡ J 6 4 3
◇ Q 2
♣ K 4 3

♠ 6 5
♡ A 10 8 2
◇ J 10 8 7
♣ Q J 6

Dummy covers with the queen and partner's king wins the trick. Partner switches to the nine of clubs, taken in dummy with the king. The ace and king of spades follow, partner playing the four and the ten. Dummy leads the diamond two to partner's ace and he continues with the two of clubs. Declarer rises with the ace and exits with the club ten to my queen, partner playing the seven. I now have my first real decision of the hand. Should I break the heart suit or should I lead a diamond, perhaps conceding a sluff and ruff.

What is known so far?

Declarer is known to hold five spades, AJxxx, as partner would have echoed with three. He also has Axx in clubs. Partner has played the 9,2,7 and would not have been in such a rush to lead them unless he held the eight as well. Even if he had switched to clubs from 972 he would have played them 9,7,2 rather than 9,2,7. If partner hasn't got the eight of clubs we are going to have a little talk.

Declarer has shown up with two small diamonds and he may have one more. He won't have two more or he wouldn't have drawn trump with such abandon.

And finally, since declarer refused the invitation, he doesn't have both the king and queen of hearts.

With all this in mind, what is the best play?

Trusting that I have the correct count of the hand, I exit with the ten of diamonds.

Declarer's possible distributions are: 5-2-3-3 and 5-3-2-3.

If declarer has the first shape he will ruff the diamond in dummy and lead a heart. The defense will come to two heart tricks regardless of declarer's play, assuming that partner has one of the missing heart honors.

If declarer has the second shape, he will get a sluff and a ruff and will shed one of his three hearts. But he will still have two hearts to lose.

In practice, declarer gets the sluff and ruff, but when he leads a heart to his king we take my ace and partner's queen.

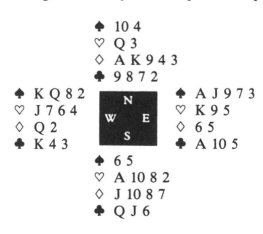

♠ 10 4
♡ Q 3
♢ A K 9 4 3
♣ 9 8 7 2

♠ K Q 8 2   ♠ A J 9 7 3
♡ J 7 6 4   ♡ K 9 5
♢ Q 2   ♢ 6 5
♣ K 4 3   ♣ A 10 5

♠ 6 5
♡ A 10 8 2
♢ J 10 8 7
♣ Q J 6

Partner's club shift was necessary. Without it, declarer would have had time to establish a heart trick for a club discard.

FURTHER ANALYSIS

Many players give a trump echo only when hoping for a ruff. It is my belief that you should give one any time you have three trumps to help partner count the hand. You might refrain if you thought it would help declarer guess the trump suit. But in most other cases it will be more useful to partner to know you have a third trump than to declarer to know that you are specifically the defender who has it. Often declarer will play off two high trumps, leaving one outstanding, and it is useful for the defense to know whether declarer was on a nine-card fit as opposed to an eight-card fit.

If I had thought declarer had four clubs, I would have played the ace of hearts when in with the club queen. A sluff-ruff would be bad defense against a 5-2-2-4 shape. It is important that partner and I be on the same wave length. Here I was able to trust partner to have four clubs and could defend accordingly.

21

♠ A 8 4 2
♡ K 9 6 3
◇ 9 5
♣ 8 5 2

With no one vulnerable, the bidding starts briskly with ONE CLUB by LHO and a cheerful THREE NOTRUMP by responder. Opener rebids FOUR CLUBS, also sounding cheerful and my RHO volunteers that this is asking for aces. RHO answers FOUR SPADES. I suppose I could whack this but I think I would prefer a heart lead if LHO is going to declare. When LHO, sounding a little less cheerful now, bids SIX CLUBS, the auction is over and partner leads the diamond jack.

Dealer: West
Vul: Both

WEST	NORTH	EAST	SOUTH
1 ♣	Pass	3 NT	Pass
4 ♣	Pass	4 ♠	Pass
6 ♣	Pass	Pass	Pass

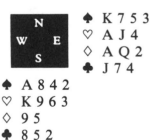

♠ K 7 5 3
♡ A J 4
◇ A Q 2
♣ J 7 4

♠ A 8 4 2
♡ K 9 6 3
◇ 9 5
♣ 8 5 2

Declarer begins by telling partner that three notrump was a terrible bid. Not enough points, four card major...oh, woe is me.

This little speech is encouraging, especially as I don't think this opponent is devious enough to be doing it on purpose. However I have heard opponents complain before when their contract was actually cold. They were just bad dummy players and had no clue.

The one thing I have learned from this is not to let these laments relax me to the point of losing my concentration. It may be a bad contract, but that doesn't mean it's hopeless.

Declarer wins the king of diamonds as I give count with the nine, and plays ace, king and a club to dummy's jack. Partner followed once and then pitched the diamond eight and the heart two. From this I assume partner started with five diamonds and unspecified major suit shape. When dummy leads the spade three I have to decide whether to rise. If declarer has the stiff queen of spades, I should take this trick.

Is this likely?

If declarer has the stiff queen, then partner has J1096 and might have led one rather than a diamond. True, partner might have been swayed by the fact that I did not double four spades, so there may be less to my analysis than I think.

Can declarer be void?

No. Then partner would have QJ1096 of spades and would surely have led one.

I do duck and declarer plays the queen and partner the six. Declarer enters dummy with a diamond and leads the spade five.

What now?

This is easier. If declarer has the queen and jack of spades he has twelve tricks via two spades, one heart, three diamonds and six clubs. So I duck again. Partner takes declarer's nine with his ten and returns the jack of spades. Declarer ruffs and takes the heart finesse. One down.

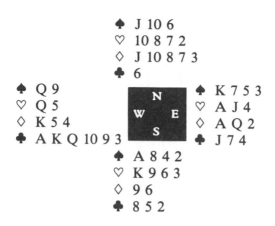

```
                    ♠ J 10 6
                    ♡ 10 8 7 2
                    ◊ J 10 8 7 3
                    ♣ 6
    ♠ Q 9                         ♠ K 7 5 3
    ♡ Q 5          N              ♡ A J 4
    ◊ K 5 4      W   E            ◊ A Q 2
    ♣ A K Q 10 9 3  S             ♣ J 7 4
                    ♠ A 8 4 2
                    ♡ K 9 6 3
                    ◊ 9 6
                    ♣ 8 5 2
```

It would have been easier with a heart lead! I also note that the contract was hardly as bad as it sounded when the declarer saw the dummy.

FURTHER ANALYSIS

It is useful to be able to exchange information regarding suit length. On this hand partner led the diamond jack and later discarded the eight. I commented that this showed a five card suit. While there are other methods, we play something called present count where your discard shows the present number of cards held.

i.e.:

J10872   Lead the jack and discard the eight, showing an even number of cards at the time of the discard.

J108752   Lead the jack and discard the two, implying an odd number of cards held now.

J1082   Lead the jack and discard the two. Partner will have to decide whether you started with four or six. This is easier for him than an uneducated guess as to whether you have four, five or six.

Note that the heart deuce could not be treated as showing count. When you are under pressure, you sometimes have to give up an exchange of information in favor of finding a safe discard.

22

♠ 9 8 4 3 2
♡ 6
◊ A Q 7 4 3
♣ 10 8

No one is vul and when RHO passes I do also. The auction picks up steam now as LHO opens ONE HEART and gets FOUR HEARTS from his partner. Everyone is content and partner leads the diamond jack.

Dealer: East
Vul: None

EAST	SOUTH	WEST	NORTH
Pass	Pass	1 ♡	Pass
4 ♡	Pass	Pass	Pass

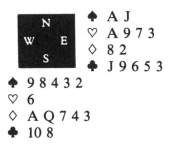

♠ A J
♡ A 9 7 3
◊ 8 2
♣ J 9 6 5 3

♠ 9 8 4 3 2
♡ 6
◊ A Q 7 4 3
♣ 10 8

This doesn't look like much of a four heart bid, but since we haven't set it yet, I better reserve judgment. At trick one I win the ace as declarer plays the six. We play that the jack denies a higher honor, so I can place declarer with the king. I shift to the club ten and declarer plays the king. It wasn't too smooth though and everyone knows it wasn't a stiff. Partner wins the ace, cashes the club queen and then shifts to the spade six. Declarer grabs the ace and leads the club jack.

What's going on? What is the right defense?

What's going on is that declarer is almost surely missing either the king or queen of trump. With solid trumps he would draw them and run the club suit. By playing in this fashion he is clearly "fishing" for help in the trump suit. My choices are to ruff or not to ruff and I can't see ruffing when declarer is trying to get me to do just that. I pitch a spade instead. Declarer pitches a spade as well and tries again with the nine of clubs. If I'm going to be consistent, I'm not going to ruff this either. I pitch another spade and declarer pitches the spade queen. Dummy facetiously proffers the last club but declarer waves it off. Instead he leads to his king of diamonds and ruffs a diamond. I follow with the seven and the queen. Finally declarer plays the ace and another heart. When I show out, he concedes one down.

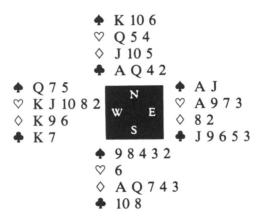

                    ♠ K 10 6
                    ♡ Q 5 4
                    ◇ J 10 5
                    ♣ A Q 4 2
    ♠ Q 7 5   ♠ A J
    ♡ K J 10 8 2   N   ♡ A 9 7 3
    ◇ K 9 6   W   E   ◇ 8 2
    ♣ K 7   S   ♣ J 9 6 5 3
                    ♠ 9 8 4 3 2
                    ♡ 6
                    ◇ A Q 7 4 3
                    ♣ 10 8

The main point of this hand is that when someone tries to get you to do something, it is usually best not to do it. If declarer could draw trump, he would. When he didn't, he couldn't.

23

♠ 8 7 5
♡ Q J 10 6 3
◇ J 4
♣ 9 7 6

Vul vs not, my partner passes. This does not look good for our side. RHO is busy counting up his points and finally emerges with ONE DIAMOND. If we weren't vul, I would liven things up with two hearts, but under the circumstances I have to pass. LHO bids ONE SPADE and opener bids a prompt TWO NOTRUMP. Responder raises to FOUR NOTRUMP and opener confidently contracts for SIX NOTRUMP. Responder looks annoyed and bids SEVEN NOTRUMP.

Dealer: North
Vul: North-South

NORTH	EAST	SOUTH	WEST
Pass	1 ◇	Pass	1 ♠
Pass	2 NT	Pass	4 NT
Pass	6 NT	Pass	7 NT
Pass	Pass	Pass	

The one good thing about this hand is that I have an easy lead. I lead the queen of hearts and see this dummy. I wonder what in the world dummy was thinking.

♠ K 9 6 3
♡ 8 5 4
◇ A Q 5
♣ K J 3

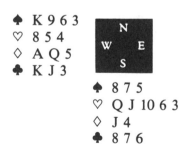

♠ 8 7 5
♡ Q J 10 6 3
◇ J 4
♣ 8 7 6

The heart queen goes to the four, two and declarer's ace. Next comes a diamond to dummy's ace and then the queen, partner playing the two and seven. At trick four declarer leads a spade to his jack and looks quite pleased with himself when it wins. He follows with the ace of spades on which partner drops the queen! The king of diamonds now and I pitch a heart, partner playing the nine of diamonds.

Declarer still seems fairly happy about things and, after some thought, bangs down the king of hearts.

What's going on? Are we going to beat this?

As to the first question, declarer almost surely has twelve tricks, three spades, two hearts, five diamonds and two clubs. His thirteenth trick could come from a club finesse, but if that were his only option, he would take that finesse now instead of setting up our hearts and risking two down. The line he is taking almost certainly means that he hopes for four spade tricks and this means he has AJx. If he had AJ10, he would have tried the finesse again.

Therefore, it is possible to reconstruct declarer's hand almost exactly. It is:

♠ AJx
♡ AK
◇ K10xxx
♣ Axx

He is going to cash out his winners and hope the spades are worth four tricks. If he continues as I expect, dummy will come down to:

♠ K9
♣ J

and will decide whether to finesse against my ten or play for the drop, hoping partner has it.

Therefore, the one thing I must not do is throw a spade or retain a card I am known to have.

Thus, on the king of hearts, I discard the ten of hearts. The king and ace of clubs and another diamond follow. On the diamond I can afford my last small club, and, since this would be my natural discard holding two spades and a high heart as well, I choose it. When the last diamond is led this is the actual situation:

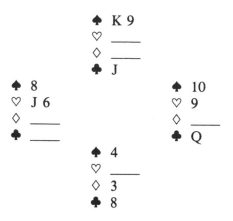

and this is the situation I hope declarer decides actually exists:

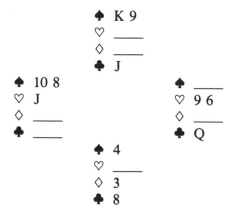

In order to encourage this misconception I drop the jack of hearts. Dummy discards the club jack and partner the nine of hearts.

Now when declarer leads his four of spades he has a difficult decision, and ultimately goes wrong, losing the last two tricks.

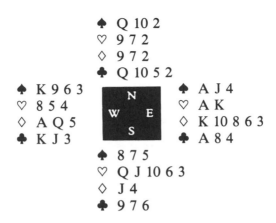

Note that once declarer's line become clear, it was necessary for the defense to create an appropriate illusion.

Let's say South threw away the 3,6 jack of hearts. That would mean that if he held four spades, he had led the heart queen from QJ63—most unlikely against seven notrump. Also that would leave North with 10972 of hearts and he would have encouraged at trick one rather than play the two.

Throwing the 3, 10 and jack created a picture that declarer could believe. Now South's lead from QJ103 would be normal and North's two more reasonable.

24

♠ 9 5 2
♡ Q J 2
♢ A 8
♣ K Q J 10 3

Not vul vs vul I have a routine opening bid of ONE CLUB. Partner responds ONE DIAMOND and I rebid ONE NO-TRUMP. LHO and partner pass and I wonder if I'm going to play a hand. Perhaps. RHO DOUBLES and I pass. I assume this is a penalty double but I have no reason to run. LHO does not seem to be on the same wavelength as his partner and he bids TWO CLUBS. Partner DOUBLES this. RHO passes as do I. After all how bad can this be? It gets better. LHO REDOUBLES and RHO passes either irrationally or from pique. This may be the biggest number since the Bell system first published its best seller.

Dealer: South
Vul: East-West

SOUTH	WEST	NORTH	EAST
1 ♣	Pass	1 ♢	Pass
1 NT	Pass	Pass	Double
Pass	2 ♣	Double	Pass
Pass	Redouble	Pass	Pass
Pass			

Partner leads the jack of diamonds which is a slight disappointment. I had been hoping for a trump lead.

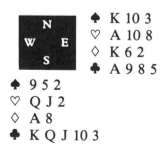

♠ K 10 3
♡ A 10 8
♢ K 6 2
♣ A 9 8 5

♠ 9 5 2
♡ Q J 2
♢ A 8
♣ K Q J 10 3

Dummy plays low and I take my ace. Since partner wouldn't lead trump, I will and I lead the ten. This is not intended as a facetious fourth best, but rather to convey to partner how good my trumps really are. Frankly I've never had quite such a pleasant problem and I don't know exactly which club to lead. I am permitted to hold the trick, as the others play the two, four and five.

What now?

For partner to double he needs fair defensive values. He can hardly have expected me to have such good clubs so his values must include almost all the remaining high cards. Thus, since his diamonds are headed by the jack, he must have the heart king and the spade ace, and I would expect him to have the spade queen as well, although he might have only the jack. Maybe he has both.

While it looks easy to continue clubs, that may cause some embarrassment for partner. I don't know for sure that he has a stiff club, but that possibility exists. Maybe I can hold momentarily on the trumps and firm up the defensive communications.

How can I do that?

At trick three I switch to the queen of hearts. If partner has three hearts, this switch won't make much difference, but if he has four, then he will recognize them as winners and will hold them if possible.

The heart queen wins also and now I can get back to clubs. I lead the king which declarer elects to take. Partner, who had a singleton club, discards a high spade.

Declarer comes to hand with the queen of diamonds and leads the seven of spades to dummy's ten, as partner completes an echo. Now declarer tries to cash the diamond king but I ruff, draw trump, and continue with the jack of hearts. We now have tricks to burn and the result is a satisfying 2200.

79

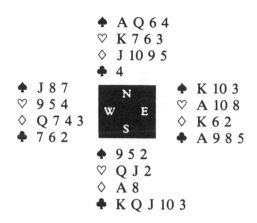

♠ A Q 6 4
♡ K 7 6 3
◇ J 10 9 5
♣ 4

♠ J 8 7   ♠ K 10 3
♡ 9 5 4   ♡ A 10 8
◇ Q 7 4 3   ◇ K 6 2
♣ 7 6 2   ♣ A 9 8 5

♠ 9 5 2
♡ Q J 2
◇ A 8
♣ K Q J 10 3

FURTHER ANALYSIS

Defense is a delicate matter of communication and timing. On this hand, North might have discarded hearts and diamonds, hoping South had the spade jack. If this were so then North's spades could be set up. Clearing up the heart situation early enabled North to discard to best advantage.

After the first trick, North should know South is 3-3-2-5 because:
    1. South would rebid a major suit instead of one notrump if he had a four card major.
    2. South would not take the ace of diamonds if he had three of them.
It is barely possible that South is 3-2-2-6 but that would be a bonus.

25

♠ 3
♡ 10 7 5
◊ A J 10 9 8 3
♣ J 10 3

Not vul vs vul, my partner opens ONE SPADE. I respond ONE NOTRUMP and LHO's TWO HEART overcall is passed back to me. With an eye on the vulnerability I venture THREE DIAMONDS. This is passed around to my RHO and he competes with THREE HEARTS which ends the auction.

Dealer: North
Vul: East-West

NORTH	EAST	SOUTH	WEST
1 ♠	Pass	1 NT	2 ♡
Pass	Pass	3 ◊	Pass
Pass	3 ♡	Pass	

Partner leads the king of diamonds and a rather good dummy appears.

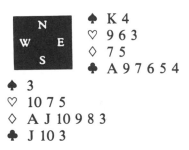

♠ K 4
♡ 9 6 3
◊ 7 5
♣ A 9 7 6 5 4

♠ 3
♡ 10 7 5
◊ A J 10 9 8 3
♣ J 10 3

What should be the defensive plan? For starters, if I wish I can overtake the king of diamonds and return my stiff spade. Should I?

This is easy to reject because partner might have either Kx or a singleton. Therefore I encourage and partner continues with the queen. This time it is safe to overtake and I do. It looks automatic to return the three of spades but I'm not so sure it's right. I may be able to get a ruff but it may be that I end up ruffing a loser.

What is declarer's shape?

Even though partner would not necessarily rebid two spades with a six card suit, his pass to two hearts tends to suggest only five spades. This means declarer has possibly five spades, five hearts, two diamonds and one card unaccounted for. I tend to think the thirteenth card is a club, but have no guarantee.

Since declarer will have to play spades, I don't see any reason to start them myself, so I exit with a trump. Declarer wins the king and plays a spade to dummy's king. Dummy returns the four of spades and I have to decide whether to ruff.

Should I?

Probably not, the reason is that if I ruff, I will be ruffing a loser. Declarer will draw another round of trump and then be able to ruff a spade in dummy safely.

I pitch a diamond on the spade and declarer wins the ace and ruffs a spade. Partner so far has played the two, queen and nine of spades. I assume this shows that his suit is solid after the ace and king. Dummy ruffs with the nine and I overruff with the ten. It probably doesn't matter what I do but I choose to exit with my last heart. Declarer wins the ace, felling partner's jack and he concedes two further spades for down one.

The full hand turns out to be approximately as anticipated:

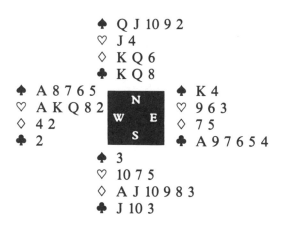

```
              ♠ Q J 10 9 2
              ♡ J 4
              ◇ K Q 6
              ♣ K Q 8
  ♠ A 8 7 6 5           ♠ K 4
  ♡ A K Q 8 2    N      ♡ 9 6 3
  ◇ 4 2       W     E   ◇ 7 5
  ♣ 2            S      ♣ A 9 7 6 5 4
              ♠ 3
              ♡ 10 7 5
              ◇ A J 10 9 8 3
              ♣ J 10 3
```

Ruffing the second spade would have cost the setting trick. If left to his own devices declarer could get five hearts, two spades, and a club, but could not ruff a spade because it would be over-ruffed. If the defense ruffed that second round of spades it would have lost the ability to score that overruff. This is a common defensive situation, which should be thoroughly understood.

FURTHER ANALYSIS

Let's say the play went slightly differently. Diamond king, diamond to the ace, and a heart shift to the ace. Now say declarer tried the line of club ace, club ruff, spade king and club ruff, setting up the club suit and a second round of trump followed by the ace of spades.

This would be the position:

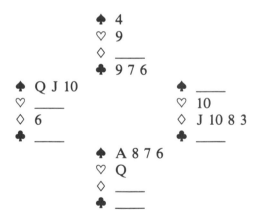

East must refuse to ruff this. Now declarer cannot get to, and use, the good clubs in dummy.

This principle of not ruffing a loser is a sound one and, more often than not, it will see you through successfully. But there are exceptions. If, for instance, you cannot overruff the dummy, you might decide to ignore principle and take the trick instead. For instance:

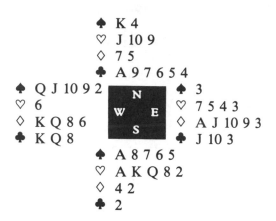

♠ K 4
♡ J 10 9
◇ 7 5
♣ A 9 7 6 5 4

♠ Q J 10 9 2
♡ 6
◇ K Q 8 6
♣ K Q 8

♠ 3
♡ 7 5 4 3
◇ A J 10 9 3
♣ J 10 3

♠ A 8 7 6 5
♡ A K Q 8 2
◇ 4 2
♣ 2

In this setting, after two rounds of diamonds and a trump shift, East would do well to ruff the second spade and return another trump. Declarer will come to one ruff in dummy rather than two. It is very worthwhile to compare this situation to the primary hand in this group.

26

♠ 9 4 3
♡ 9 2
◇ A Q J 6 3
♣ A 8 6

I am playing in a matchpoint event against excellent opponents, and my vulnerable LHO opens ONE SPADE. We are not vulnerable and under the circumstances my partner is sometimes inclined to extravagances. When he makes a weak jump overcall of THREE HEARTS and RHO passes, it does not occur to me to bid. Opposite my partner's jump overcalls two aces and two trumps may hold it to down two. When I pass, LHO rebids THREE NOTRUMP which is passed back to me. It might be right to double, but I expect that if it goes down we will get a good result. Double would get a heart lead for sure, but if I pass, partner may decide to lead something else. Who knows, he might lead a diamond.

He doesn't. He leads the two of clubs, and a very good dummy comes down.

Dealer: West
Vul: East-West

WEST	NORTH	EAST	SOUTH
1 ♠	3 ♡	Pass	Pass
3 NT	Pass	Pass	Pass

♠ 10 2
♡ A 10 8
◇ K 10 4 2
♣ 10 9 5 3

♠ 9 4 3
♡ 9 2
◇ A Q J 6 3
♣ A 8 6

I win the ace and declarer drops the jack. I expect partner has either the king or queen of clubs, or else he would not have led low.

What shall I do now?

What are my options?

I seem to have three, and none of them look good. I can shift to a heart, I can return a club, or I can lead back the jack or queen of diamonds. A spade somehow doesn't seem right.

What in the world is going on? Where did declarer find a three notrump bid? What can he have?

For starters, he does have something in hearts. Looking at this dummy, I would expect declarer to have Kx, perhaps Qx, or maybe even a stiff king of hearts. He has nothing in diamonds and either KJ(x) or QJ(x) of clubs. The only thing of value he can have is a slew of spades which he hopes to run. From my point of view they will run and the only problem is to cash out as many tricks as possible. I doubt we can beat this, but perhaps four spades will make.

I don't think a diamond return best because we will probably get only two tricks in the suit whether I lead them or partner does. I would prefer to get our tricks without declarer getting one.

So will it be a heart or a club?

I finally decide on a club. I expect that partner will get in with a club eventually and will wonder why I returned a club as opposed to a heart. I hope he will judge to return a diamond rather than a heart.

Whether or not there is anything to all of this, when I return the eight to declarer's four and partner's king, he does return the nine of diamonds. I win dummy's ten with my jack.

Has declarer blocked the club suit? Should I exit with a heart to knock out dummy's entry?

Almost certainly not. I cash the ace of diamonds as declarer shows out. In the same motion he tables his cards and claims.

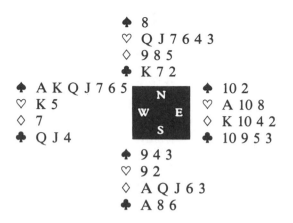

```
              ♠ 8
              ♡ Q J 7 6 4 3
              ◇ 9 8 5
              ♣ K 7 2
♠ A K Q J 7 6 5    ┌─────┐    ♠ 10 2
♡ K 5              │  N  │    ♡ A 10 8
◇ 7                │W   E│    ◇ K 10 4 2
♣ Q J 4            │  S  │    ♣ 10 9 5 3
                   └─────┘
              ♠ 9 4 3
              ♡ 9 2
              ◇ A Q J 6 3
              ♣ A 8 6
```

A heart return at trick two would have given partner a harder time of it. Declarer would win the king and lead the four of clubs. Now North would have to rise and then resist the urge to lead the queen of hearts.

FURTHER ANALYSIS

A heart return would be necessary if declarer had the Q5 instead of the K5. As against that holding, he might have held the club KJ(x) instead of the auction QJ(x). As enterprising as this player is, I don't think he would venture three notrump with two and a half unstopped suits. As it is, it was exciting and he must have awaited the dummy with some anticipation. I can only hope enough people reach four spades to make our defense worthwhile.

27

♠ A J 3
♡ 2
◇ J 9 6 3 2
♣ J 10 8 4

Not vul vs vul the bidding begins with ONE SPADE by LHO. My partner overcalls TWO HEARTS and I am pleased to hear RHO bid TWO SPADES. As much as I like to compete against fit auctions this hand is not sufficient. A responsive double is a possible action, but with seventy percent of my values in their suit, and poor shape, this hand is too thin. I pass, as does opener, and partner contemplates but can't come up with anything. Two spades becomes the final contract.

Dealer: West
Vul: East-West

WEST	NORTH	EAST	SOUTH
1 ♠	2 ♡	2 ♠	Pass
Pass	Pass		

Partner's lead is the heart king.

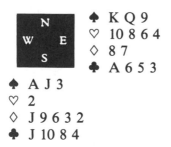

♠ K Q 9
♡ 10 8 6 4
◇ 8 7
♣ A 6 5 3

♠ A J 3
♡ 2
◇ J 9 6 3 2
♣ J 10 8 4

The heart king wins and partner continues with the heart queen and ace. I follow once and discard the two and three of diamonds. Declarer follows with the three, jack and seven. Partner continues with the nine of hearts to dummy's ten. I have to decide whether to trump this or discard.

As usual, it would be nice to know what is going on, but I think I can make a fairly accurate reconstruction.

Partner has five hearts exactly, to the AKQ. He does not have another five card suit because he would almost never sell out to two spades. If he had another five card suit he would bid it knowing he could count on me to have some values. Also, partner doesn't have a singleton spade because he would have reopened with a double.

For instance, with:

♠ x
♡ AKQxx
♢ 10xx
♣ Kxxx

he would reopen with a double, showing probably a 1-5-4-3, 1-5-3-4, 1-6-3-3, or perhaps a 2-5-3-3 hand. Only with the latter shape would he need more than a minimum overcall for a reopening double.

When the opponents have a fit, it doesn't pay to go quietly. Partner knows this, and I know he won't quit on any hand which could continue.

Therefore, since partner did not compete, he does not have a second five card suit, and he does not have a stiff spade.

The nine of hearts is suit preference, suggesting a diamond return, but looking at the dummy, I don't think this means very much. Partner can't really have good enough clubs to request a club return, so he would request a diamond even if he didn't want it.

If two spades can be set, how do we go about it? And, of immediate concern, what should I play at trick four?

We have five visible tricks in the form of two spades and three hearts, so one trick in minors will suffice, in spite of this enormous dummy. I can proceed in one of three ways:

1. I can discard on the heart and hope we come to three additional tricks.

2. I can ruff with the jack.

3. I can ruff with the three.

Which is it?

Curiously, the play that has the most appeal is the third play, ruffing with the three.

Why is this apparent sacrifice of a trump trick the best defense?

I don't claim that this must be the best defense. It may permit them to make three spades, or it may cost the setting trick when either of the alternative plays would work. As against these possibilities however are weighed the possibility that declarer will overruff, but subsequently misguess in trump and lose two trump tricks anyway! If we have a minor suit trick coming, we will still get it as declarer won't get to use the ten of hearts for a discard.

Possible hands for declarer are:

♠ 10xxxx	♠ 10xxxx	♠ 10xxxx
♡ Jxx	♡ Jxx	♡ Jxx
◇ AQx	◇ AK	◇ AKQ
♣ KQ	♣ Kxx	♣ Qx

Given that declarer has only five poor spades, it is hard to find one where we can beat two spades if declarer can discard on the ten of hearts. True, on the first of these three hands, we can beat two spades if I ruff with the jack and return a diamond. But we can't beat it if I discard.

I do ruff with the three which is overruffed with the four. Now the spade two to the five, king and my ace. I return the six of diamonds to the queen and king. We now have book. If partner leads a heart, I can score my jack of spades because I am ruffing after dummy. The old uppercut.

Will partner work it out?

Yes. He does return the heart five. Declarer looks at me and shrugs. I show him the jack of spades and he shows his hand conceding down one.

The complete hand:

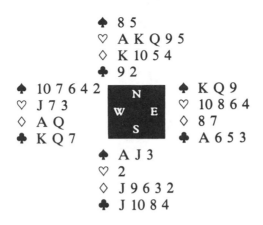

♠ 8 5
♡ A K Q 9 5
◇ K 10 5 4
♣ 9 2

♠ 10 7 6 4 2   ♠ K Q 9
♡ J 7 3   ♡ 10 8 6 4
◇ A Q   ◇ 8 7
♣ K Q 7   ♣ A 6 5 3

♠ A J 3
♡ 2
◇ J 9 6 3 2
♣ J 10 8 4

A lot happened on this hand. In the end game, partner was able to judge that I could not hold sufficient high cards to get a club trick, but it was possible that I had the jack of spades. Declarer might or might not have guessed the position, but this way he had no chance.

FURTHER ANALYSIS

Declarer had quite a few options in the play including refusing the diamond finesse. He could then try to guess the spades, or he could simply play to the queen and then hope to find clubs three-three.

28

♠ 7 5 2
♡ K 10 8 3
♢ Q 10 3
♣ Q 10 3

With no one vul, RHO opens ONE SPADE. I pass and LHO raises to TWO SPADES. Partner DOUBLES and RHO continues to THREE SPADES. LHO alerts this. I ask and am told three spades is not forward going. I have a useful hand, but I don't think enough of it to venture out at the four level so I pass. Perhaps partner can double again. Some players would bid four hearts here hoping to stampede the opponents into four spades, and might succeed. This works both ways however. Just because three spades is weak doesn't mean my hand is any better and I refuse to allow them to stampede me into four hearts.

All my thoughts go for naught because LHO bids FOUR SPADES. This is unexpected and everyone at the table looks up in surprise.

Surprised or not, partner passes as do I. Just because you don't like the opponents' bidding is no reason to double them. Now we have to beat them.

Dealer: East
Vul: None

EAST	SOUTH	WEST	NORTH
1 ♠	Pass	2 ♠	Double
3 ♠	Pass	4 ♠	Pass
Pass	Pass		

I'm not sure why LHO would go on to game after a sign off. My guess is he has some distributional quirk. Since I am not immediately afraid of dummy coming down with a good side suit, I lead the spade five.

♠ K Q 6
♡ 9 7 4
◇ A 9 7 6 2
♣ 7 6

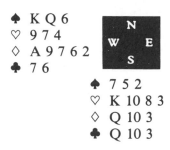

♠ 7 5 2
♡ K 10 8 3
◇ Q 10 3
♣ Q 10 3

Dummy wins the king, partner following with the four. Declarer discards the heart two on dummy's ace of diamonds and leads a small club. Partner rises with the king of clubs and returns the eight of spades. Declarer wins with the nine in hand and leads a small club towards dummy's seven spot.

What's going on here?

At this stage it is pretty easy to reconstruct the distribution. Partner has shown up with two spades and five diamonds. The rest of his shape should be three-three. If he has four hearts, then he has only two clubs. If this is the case, then declarer is 5-2-0-6. This is both unlikely and unbeatable.

The high cards are also easy to locate. Partner is marked with the KJ of diamonds and the AK of clubs. He probably has a higher heart honor, else his double would be dangerous, especially if he has three poor hearts. Declarer therefore has something like:

♠ AJ109x
♡ Axx
◇ ——
♣ xxxxx

and the defense will be easy. Win the club, return the last trump, and eventually come to a heart trick plus another club trick.

Is this all there is to the hand?

Almost. There is one last hurdle.

And that is?

If partner's clubs are AKJ, it is necessary to rise with the queen of clubs. If not, partner will win the trick and the defense will not be able to get in that third round of trump.

Trusting that my picture of the hand is not in error, I play the club queen, curious to see if it was necessary. Partner plays the jack. It was necessary. I lead my last spade and when clubs are three-three, declarer concedes down one.

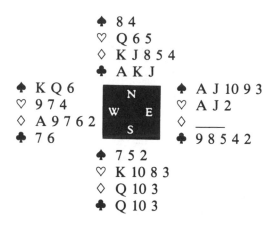

        ♠ 8 4
        ♡ Q 6 5
        ◇ K J 8 5 4
        ♣ A K J
♠ K Q 6   ♠ A J 10 9 3
♡ 9 7 4   ♡ A J 2
◇ A 9 7 6 2   ◇ ——
♣ 7 6   ♣ 9 8 5 4 2
        ♠ 7 5 2
        ♡ K 10 8 3
        ◇ Q 10 3
        ♣ Q 10 3

FURTHER ANALYSIS

Declarer might have won the second round of spades in the dummy in order to lead the second club. Now partner would have to play the jack!, hoping I had the queen and would overtake to lead the last trump. Or alternatively, declarer could win the first trump in hand and lead a club. Now the winning defense would be for partner to win the king, rather than the jack, thus preserving my entry in clubs. LHO should not have bid four spades. If you trust partner to know what he is doing, you should respect his opinion, maximum raise notwithstanding.

29

♠ 9 2
♡ Q 8 6 2
♢ A Q 9
♣ A Q 6 3

No one is vulnerable and in spite of my good hand the opponents bid briskly to game. LHO starts with ONE SPADE and they bid thusly:

LHO	RHO
1 ♠	2 ♢
2 ♠	4 ♠

Partner leads the three of diamonds.

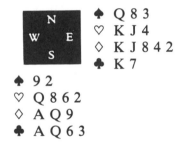

♠ Q 8 3
♡ K J 4
♢ K J 8 4 2
♣ K 7

♠ 9 2
♡ Q 8 6 2
♢ A Q 9
♣ A Q 6 3

Dummy plays low and I win the queen as declarer plays the ten. This is somewhat suspicious. I don't think my partner would lead the three of diamonds from 7653 of a suit bid by dummy. I am pretty sure partner has led a stiff. Declarer probably has a minimum opener and did not want to raise diamonds. My hand seems to confirm this. There are only thirteen missing points.

At trick two I cash the ace of diamonds and partner discards the club two. So much for declarer's false card.

What now? Should I give partner his ruff?

It looks safe to do this. Partner will ruff and return a club. Probably down two.

Right?

Perhaps. It is easy to wish that partner will return a club, but in the real world, partner may think the nine of diamonds is suit preference for hearts. Partner doesn't know, as I do, that declarer has four diamonds. He may think I started with, say, AQ96 and want a heart return. Certainly if my clubs and hearts were reversed, that is how I would defend.

How can partner be prevented from returning a heart?

He can't. So, for that reason, I cash the club ace before giving partner his ruff. When I see all four hands, it is apparent that my defense has lost a trick theoretically, but probably was necessary to defeat four spades.

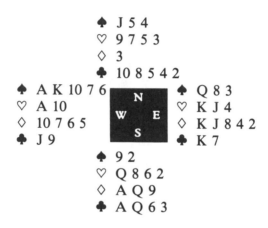

```
                 ♠ J 5 4
                 ♡ 9 7 5 3
                 ◇ 3
                 ♣ 10 8 5 4 2
   ♠ A K 10 7 6          ♠ Q 8 3
   ♡ A 10         N       ♡ K J 4
   ◇ 10 7 6 5   W   E     ◇ K J 8 4 2
   ♣ J 9           S      ♣ K 7
                 ♠ 9 2
                 ♡ Q 8 6 2
                 ◇ A Q 9
                 ♣ A Q 6 3
```

FURTHER ANALYSIS

This type of play is known as building a fence around partner. It is needed when one member of the partnership can see the winning defense and can tell that this defense may not be apparent to partner. Under these circumstances you, or partner, may take over the defense, even at the cost of a trick when that action is sure to beat the contract. This is what happened on the hand being discussed. Partner may claim that he would not have done the wrong thing, but you can be sure he will appreciate not having to face the problem.

30

♠ 9 5 3
♡ A 10 9 3
◇ K 8 3
♣ A Q 3

We are vul against not vul and RHO opens ONE CLUB. At any other vulnerability I might double, but, as it is, I pass. LHO jumps to TWO NOTRUMP and opener raises to THREE NOTRUMP.

Dealer: East
Vul: North-South

EAST	SOUTH	WEST	NORTH
1 ♣	Pass	2 NT	Pass
3 NT	Pass	Pass	Pass

Partner selects the heart four and dummy appears. I ask if two notrump was forcing. It was. 12-14 HCP's.

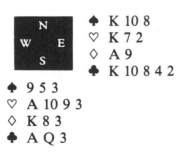

♠ K 10 8
♡ K 7 2
◇ A 9
♣ K 10 8 4 2

♠ 9 5 3
♡ A 10 9 3
◇ K 8 3
♣ A Q 3

At trick one dummy plays the two of hearts. The standard play is the nine. If partner is leading from the jack, the play of the nine will prevent declarer from taking two heart tricks and will enable us to run off the next three heart tricks when partner gets in.

Is this the correct play?

Perhaps. Perhaps not. Is partner going to get in?

Not likely. If declarer has the range ascribed to him, then partner has two points at most and may have one or none. Partner's lead of a small heart suggests an honor, so he won't have anything on the side.

Is there a winning defense?

Again, perhaps. Since playing the nine cannot win, perhaps a different play will. If partner has led from the queen, then I can take the ace and return the ten, trapping declarer's hypothetical jack.

Would partner lead from Qxx against this sequence?

It is a distinct possibility. Also partner might have led from Qxxx. LHO could be a bit of a notrump hog and hold only Jx. This might not be a good bridge, but it is certainly not uncommon.

On the assumption that we cannot beat this unless partner has the queen of hearts, I take the first trick and return the ten. Declarer permits this to win and my heart continuation brings down the jack, queen and king. This results in down one, the defense taking three hearts and two clubs.

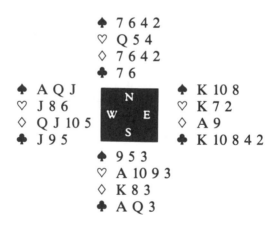

```
              ♠ 7 6 4 2
              ♡ Q 5 4
              ◊ 7 6 4 2
              ♣ 7 6
  ♠ A Q J         N         ♠ K 10 8
  ♡ J 8 6                   ♡ K 7 2
  ◊ Q J 10 5   W     E      ◊ A 9
  ♣ J 9 5         S         ♣ K 10 8 4 2
              ♠ 9 5 3
              ♡ A 10 9 3
              ◊ K 8 3
              ♣ A Q 3
```

I'm not sure I would have found partner's heart lead. But then I have no honest opinion as to what is best. The heart lead was an effort to find my long suit. Maybe there is something to this. I'm not sure.

31

♠ J 7 2
♡ A 8 7 4 2
♦ A K 10 6
♣ 10

Vulnerable vs not, the bidding is ONE SPADE, pass, ONE
NOTRUMP up to me. It could be right to act, but the J72 of
spades is a distinct minus and the lack of heart spots is another.
I pass and when opener rebids TWO HEARTS, I feel a bit better. RHO prefers to TWO SPADES and this ends the auction.

Dealer: West
Vul: North-South

WEST	NORTH	EAST	SOUTH
1 ♠	Pass	1 NT	Pass
2 ♡	Pass	2 ♠	Pass
Pass	Pass		

Partner leads the nine of spades.

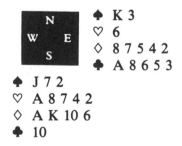

♠ K 3
♡ 6
♦ 8 7 5 4 2
♣ A 8 6 5 3

♠ J 7 2
♡ A 8 7 4 2
♦ A K 10 6
♣ 10

This looks like a good lead for us.

Not surprisingly, declarer wins dummy's king and leads the
heart six. This is a common defensive position and I must decide
whether to take the ace of hearts or duck.

Which is better?

In general, it is best to duck in this situation and since I see no
reason to go against that general principle, I do duck. I hope I
was smooth enough to give declarer a problem if he has a guess.

It appears that I have not given declarer a clue because he plays the jack, losing to partner's queen. Partner continues with another trump and we ultimately score three hearts, two diamonds and a club.

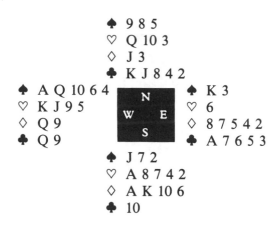

```
                    ♠ 9 8 5
                    ♡ Q 10 3
                    ◇ J 3
                    ♣ K J 8 4 2
     ♠ A Q 10 6 4                    ♠ K 3
     ♡ K J 9 5        N              ♡ 6
     ◇ Q 9         W     E           ◇ 8 7 5 4 2
     ♣ Q 9            S              ♣ A 7 6 5 3
                    ♠ J 7 2
                    ♡ A 8 7 4 2
                    ◇ A K 10 6
                    ♣ 10
```

FURTHER ANALYSIS

The obvious and significant point of this hand is the advisability of ducking an ace when dummy on your right leads its singleton.

It is worth looking at a number of examples to see the effect of ducking in such a situation:

```
           6
Q103            A8742
         KJ95
```

In this example from the hand being discussed, dummy has only one trump. If RHO takes his ace and returns a trump, the defense will take two tricks in this suit. If RHO ducks and declarer guesses correctly, playing the king, and ruffs one in dummy, he still ends up losing two tricks. And if declarer finesses the jack, he may end up losing four tricks while taking none. On this hand the defense cannot lose a trick by ducking and may gain two. Quite a difference.

Here are a few other examples. It is a very useful exercise to work out the tricks the defense wins by ducking the ace as opposed to rising with it.

Assume that dummy has one trump only in the following setups and that the defense will lead trump as soon as they get in.

A.   6   Taking the ace: One trick
                               Ducking the ace: Still one trick, as de-
        9532   A1087   clarer can ruff the four spot in dummy.

             KQJ4

B.   6   Taking the ace: Two tricks
                               Ducking the ace: Three tricks
        K983   A542

             QJ107

C.   6   Taking the ace: Two tricks
                               Ducking the ace: Two and maybe three
        J973   A542   if declarer makes the reasonable play of
                               finessing the ten.
             KQ108

D.   6   This one is the odd case where ducking
                               costs a trick. If declarer goes up with
        Q984   AJ52   the king, he gets two tricks, otherwise,
                               none.
             K1073

E.   6   Taking the ace: Three tricks
                               Ducking the ace: Likely four tricks.
        K973   A1054

             QJ82

Here is a complete hand. South plays in four spades.

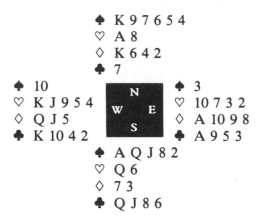

```
                    ♠ K 9 7 6 5 4
                    ♡ A 8
                    ◇ K 6 4 2
                    ♣ 7
    ♠ 10                          ♠ 3
    ♡ K J 9 5 4      N            ♡ 10 7 3 2
    ◇ Q J 5       W     E         ◇ A 10 9 8
    ♣ K 10 4 2       S            ♣ A 9 5 3
                    ♠ A Q J 8 2
                    ♡ Q 6
                    ◇ 7 3
                    ♣ Q J 8 6
```

West leads the queen of diamonds and continues with the jack. South ruffs the third round and draws trump ending in dummy. Now he plays the seven of clubs. If East rises, declarer will later lead the queen for a ruffing finesse. This will set up a club trick for a heart discard. Compare the defense if East ducks.

From a defensive point of view, you will have to consider such things as whether or not you expect the trick to come back. Does dummy have sufficient trumps to handle declarer's losers? Is your ace the only winner your side has, period?

For instance:

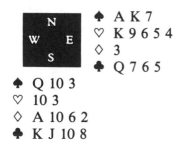

```
                    ♠ A K 7
    N               ♡ K 9 6 5 4
 W     E            ◇ 3
    S               ♣ Q 7 6 5
    ♠ Q 10 3
    ♡ 10 3
    ◇ A 10 6 2
    ♣ K J 10 8
```

After:

			You
1 ♡	Pass	3 ♡	Pass
4 ♡	Pass	Pass	Pass

Partner leads the two of spades.

Dummy wins the ace and leads its stiff diamond. It is clear to duck this. If declarer has the king and plays it you lose nothing because you will still get a spade trick. By ducking you put yourself in the running for a trick in both suits.

Deciding whether to take or duck an ace when dummy leads a stiff is a common defensive problem. Quite possibly I could fill an entire book on the subject. Perhaps someday I will. In the meantime, this one hand and the examples will have to do. For the time being, I suggest that you follow the general guideline of ducking except when you have distinct reasons for doing otherwise. Remember, the fact that dummy has a singleton is not of itself sufficient reason to take the ace. It will not take many examples to establish that ducking is far sounder than rising.

You may have a couple of ludicrous results, but the good ones will far outweigh the bad ones. Courage!

32

♠ 5 3
♡ J 10 9 5 3
◇ K J
♣ 9 7 5 3

With both sides vulnerable, the opponents are permitted a straightforward and uncontested sequence. Beginning on my right their auction is:

Dealer: East
Vul: Both

EAST	SOUTH	WEST	NORTH
1 ♠	Pass	2 ♠	Pass
3 ♠	Pass	4 ♠	Pass
Pass	Pass		

As usual I ask about three spades and am told it is a simple game try. Partner do you have a maximum? In this case West thought he did.

I have an easy choice of leads and start with the jack of hearts.

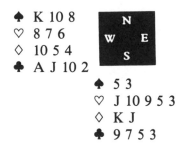

♠ K 10 8
♡ 8 7 6
◇ 10 5 4
♣ A J 10 2

♠ 5 3
♡ J 10 9 5 3
◇ K J
♣ 9 7 5 3

My lead goes to partner's ace and declarer's four. Partner's next play is little unexpected. It is the ace of diamonds! This is nice but I'm not quite sure what to do with it. I suppose I should play the jack. Partner will lead another to my king. We'll beat four spades if partner has a club or spade trick.

Is partner going to show up with an additional trick?
It's possible but not too likely. Declarer should have seventeen or so points for his game try. If he has something in this family of hands:

♠ AJxxx
♡ KQx
♢ Qxx
♣ Kx

he has a spade guess. But this hand is not really worth a game try. Perhaps declarer has the same hand with the queen of clubs.

There is something about this hand that bothers me.

What is it?

Why did partner lead the ace of diamonds rather than underlead it? He shouldn't be concerned that declarer has a stiff king for two reasons. First, this auction implies a balanced hand since otherwise declarer would have a help suit game try available. This is not guaranteed, but is a fair presumption. And secondly, if the diamond king were stiff, then I would have the QJx(x) and might have led one rather than a heart. Neither of these reasons is conclusive, but together they suggest that partner ought to be underleading the ace of diamonds.

Why didn't he do that? I suspect it is because he has the queen of diamonds. Probably he has AQxx(x) and is just cashing out. If I am right about the queen of diamonds, then partner won't have anything in clubs. He will be concerned that declarer will get some discards on the club suit.

What does this mean?

If I trust my analysis, I can play the king on the ace, permitting partner to cash the queen and give me a ruff. The more I think about it, the better I feel about these inferences. I do play the king, admittedly with some anxiety, but partner does produce the queen. Who would have thought that our defense on this hand would end with our ruffing one of declarer's diamond winners?!

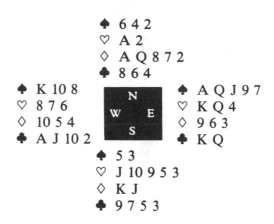

♠ 6 4 2
♡ A 2
◇ A Q 8 7 2
♣ 8 6 4

♠ K 10 8   ♠ A Q J 9 7
♡ 8 7 6   ♡ K Q 4
◇ 10 5 4   ◇ 9 6 3
♣ A J 10 2   ♣ K Q

♠ 5 3
♡ J 10 9 5 3
◇ K J
♣ 9 7 5 3

Partner's defense was well thought out. He could, if the diamond proved futile, switch back to hearts playing me for KJ10x(x).

33

♠ A 10 8 4 3
♡ Q 7
◇ A Q 5
♣ 9 7 4

We are vul versus not, and when RHO opens ONE NO-TRUMP, 15-17, I have no inclination to act. LHO bids TWO CLUBS, Stayman, and opener answers with TWO SPADES. LHO's jump to THREE NOTRUMP ends the bidding.

Dealer: East
Vul: North-South

EAST	SOUTH	WEST	NORTH
1 NT	Pass	2 ♣	Pass
2 ♠	Pass	3 NT	Pass
Pass	Pass		

LHO volunteers that they bid hearts first with both majors.

My normal lead would be the spade four, but since RHO has bid spades I may reconsider. I reject the queen of hearts because dummy should have four. If opener has three of them I will be attacking one of their seven card suits. I would far rather let them open up the suit.

Neither minor seems to be attractive. A diamond lead could work out but the bad results will be spectacular. If I lead the suit it will have to be the ace or the queen and this is just too presumptuous for me.

I'm going to lead a spade in spite of the fact that RHO has four of them. Actually, I feel rather good about this lead. Partner won't need much to help get this suit going. For instance, if this is the layout, it will be very effective, and I don't think it is asking too much to find it.

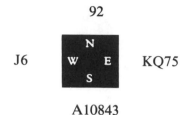

J6   KQ75

A10843

Say I lead the four and dummy wins the jack. If partner can get in, he will return the nine and I will be able to establish the suit while still holding an entry.

Can partner have an entry?

It is possible. The opponents can have as few as twenty four points which would leave partner with four. He could also have less, but there is room for something and he may get in sooner or later.

Since there are various combinations similar to the one described which will make the spade lead work, I lead the four.

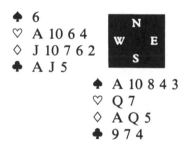

♠ 6
♡ A 10 6 4
♢ J 10 7 6 2
♣ A J 5

♠ A 10 8 4 3
♡ Q 7
♢ A Q 5
♣ 9 7 4

Trick one goes to partner's jack and declarer's king. RHO leads the club queen to the ace and partner's eight. Next comes the jack of diamonds. Partner plays the four and declarer the three.

What's up?

The play in clubs marks declarer with the KQx. Partner's eight probably shows four although he could have two. It is less clear how many diamonds partner has because he might not wish to give count. As to high cards, my estimate of partner's values has shrunk. He may have three points, but is more likely to have two. Since holding up in diamonds cannot keep declarer from setting them up, I take the queen and consider my options.

I can lead another spade, hoping partner has the queen. This is certainly possible.

I can lead another spade, hoping partner has the nine. This runs the risk of giving declarer a trick he might not get otherwise.

I can lead the heart queen, hoping partner has the king.

I can just exit with a club and play passive.

It is easy to reject the heart lead. Partner simply can't have the heart king. That would leave declarer with a fourteen point notrump.

It is also easy to reject a passive lead. Declarer will eventually set up the diamonds and will have at least nine tricks.

This leaves spades. I'm still optimistic about this suit. I don't think it's asking too much to find partner with the nine and if he happens to have the queen it would be too embarrassing for words not to lead them again.

I lead the three to partner's nine and declarer concedes defeat. We take three spades and two diamonds. One down.

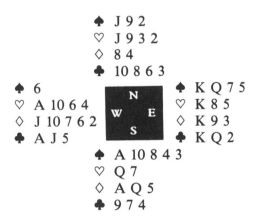

           ♠ J 9 2
           ♡ J 9 3 2
           ◇ 8 4
           ♣ 10 8 6 3

♠ 6   ♠ K Q 7 5
♡ A 10 6 4   ♡ K 8 5
◇ J 10 7 6 2   ◇ K 9 3
♣ A J 5   ♣ K Q 2

           ♠ A 10 8 4 3
           ♡ Q 7
           ◇ A Q 5
           ♣ 9 7 4

FURTHER ANALYSIS

Often when you are on lead against a notrump contract, your suit or suits have been bid by the opponents. When this happens the tendency is to look elsewhere. There is one situation in particular however where you should be fairly pleased to lead a suit bid by an opponent. This is when your RHO has bid a suit and you hold length plus an honor plus good spots. In the hand above, the spades were A10843. Had they been A6542, leading the suit would probably have been futile.

The times where this lead can be effective are when RHO has shown a probable four bagger.

Note these sequences:

1 ♣	1 ♡			1 NT		1 ♣
1 ♠	1 NT	2 ♣	2 ♡		1 ◊	1 ♡
Pass		2 NT			1 ♠	1 NT

Against these auctions you can consider leading hearts if you have something along the lines of:

A 10 8 4 3
K 10 7 6 2
Q 10 8 3
J 9 6 5 3
10 9 7 6 2

You should refrain from leading hearts if you have no spots, i.e.:

A 6 5 4 2
K 8 6 3
Q 5 3 2
J 5 4 3 2
8 7 5 3 2

This principle can be carried a bit too far. You should look elsewhere whenever RHO has shown strength or length in the suit. Against these sequences, a heart lead would be, almost by definition, a waste of time.

1 ♠	2 ♡	1 ♦	1 ♡		1 ♡*
2 ♠	2 NT	2 ♣	2 ♡	1 ♠	1 NT
3 NT		2 ♠	2 NT	3 NT	
		3 NT			

*Five card suit

One last word. If you have one of these broken holdings, and it is LHO who has bid the suit, you should again look elsewhere. The idea of leading from these suits when RHO has bid them is that you will be able to take advantage of the fact that your high cards and spots are over his. When LHO bids the suit his high cards and spots will be over yours and it will usually be an unequal struggle.

One example:

J 3

K 4   A 9 8 6

Q 10 7 5 2

J 3

A 9 8 6   K 4

Q 10 7 5 2

The first diagram is the equivalent of the suit being bid on your right. Leading the five can set up three tricks for your side.

The second diagram is the equivalent of the suit being bid on your left. Declarer will have an extra stopper which means you will be able to set up only two tricks, and you will have to work a lot harder to do it.

There is a convention which is used against notrump. You make your opening lead which declarer wins. Declarer presumedly will lead another suit. On this trick, the partner of the opening leader will play a high card in the suit being led, not to give count, but to tell the opening leader that he likes the original lead. In this hand, if my partner held QJx of spades, he would play a high club when declarer went to dummy. Had partner the J32 of spades, he would feel that it was an unexceptional holding and would play a small club instead. This convention usually applies only at trick two. I don't use it because I feel normal count is too important to give up. Nonetheless it has a significant following.

34

♠ J 10 9 7 5
♡ Q 10 4
◊ 8 7 2
♣ A 5

No one is vulnerable. There are two passes to RHO who opens ONE DIAMOND. I pass and LHO responds ONE HEART. Partner and I remain silent throughout and the opponents continue thus:

Dealer: West
Vul: None

WEST	NORTH	EAST	SOUTH
Pass	Pass	1 ◊	Pass
1 ♡	Pass	2 ♣	Pass
2 ◊	Pass	2 NT	Pass
3 NT	Pass	Pass	Pass

This sequence leaves me on lead and I am happy to have a good lead in the jack of spades.

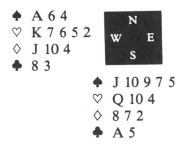

♠ A 6 4
♡ K 7 6 5 2
◊ J 10 4
♣ 8 3

♠ J 10 9 7 5
♡ Q 10 4
◊ 8 7 2
♣ A 5

I like the sequence chosen by dummy. So often I see hands like this rebid two hearts. Terrible. Of more concern I note that this contract is likely to be on the thin side. I do not like my 872 of diamonds. If declarer takes a diamond finesse, it will work.

At trick one declarer hops up with the ace of spades and partner gives me the two. When the jack of diamonds is led partner covers with the queen, losing to declarer's ace. Now comes the queen of clubs. I can take this, but should I? What do I know about the hand so far?

From the play at trick one, I think I can credit declarer with KQx of spades. Partner would be more enthusiastic with the queen. Also declarer cannot have four spades since he did not bid them. Declarer is also marked with five diamonds. If he had four my partner would have three and would not cover the diamond jack. Declarer also has four clubs. He rebid two clubs which ought to show four. With 3-2-5-3 he would either open one notrump or jump to two notrump over one heart.

Therefore declarer is almost surely 3-1-5-4. His high cards, while not yet certain, are probably

♠ KQx		♠ KQx
♡ x	or	♡ A
◇ AKxxx		◇ AKxxx
♣ KQ(J)x		♣ QJ10x

In the second case we can't beat it, but in the first case it is imperative that I take the club ace and switch to hearts. I do this and, catering to the stiff jack in declarer's hand, I lead the queen. Declarer ducks but it doesn't matter. We take four hearts plus the club ace.

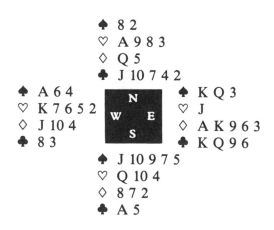

```
              ♠ 8 2
              ♡ A 9 8 3
              ◇ Q 5
              ♣ J 10 7 4 2
 ♠ A 6 4           N           ♠ K Q 3
 ♡ K 7 6 5 2   W     E         ♡ J
 ◇ J 10 4          S           ◇ A K 9 6 3
 ♣ 8 3                         ♣ K Q 9 6
              ♠ J 10 9 7 5
              ♡ Q 10 4
              ◇ 8 7 2
              ♣ A 5
```

35

♠ A J 9 7 3
♡ J 9 5
◇ 10
♣ A 7 6 5

We are vul against not vul. Partner opens ONE DIAMOND and RHO DOUBLES. I don't like it at all but our system says I must REDOUBLE, so I do. LHO bids ONE HEART and partner rebids TWO DIAMONDS. We play this shows a weakish opening bid. RHO passes and I guess to pass as well. Opposite a minimum we may be high enough in two diamonds. I might have bid two spades but that will succeed only when we have a spade fit. I judge this against the odds. LHO doesn't give up easily and contests with TWO HEARTS. My partner decides he has a good minimum and bids THREE DIAMONDS. Unbelievably, RHO is still there with THREE HEARTS. I think this joke has gone far enough and I DOUBLE. When all pass partner leads the king of diamonds.

Dealer: North
Vul: North-South

NORTH	WEST	SOUTH	EAST
1 ◇	Double	Redouble	1 ♡
2 ◇	Pass	Pass	2 ♡
3 ◇	3 ♡	Double	Pass
Pass	Pass		

♠ Q 8 5
♡ K Q 10 4
◇ 3
♣ K 10 9 8 3

♠ A J 9 7 3
♡ J 9 5
◇ 10
♣ A 7 6 5

Partner wins the first trick and switches to the king and two of spades. When dummy plays low, I win the jack. Presuming partner has two spades, we have a minimum of one down with three spades, a diamond and a club.

Can we do better?

Yes. If partner can be persuaded to lead another diamond it will promote a trump trick for my J95.

How can I get partner in?

By leading back the nine of spades. Partner will ruff and will surely know I have underled the ace of spades for a good reason. If I do this and don't get a diamond lead, I will feel disappointed.

Before doing this, I check to see if there is anything better. For instance, could partner be ruffing clubs? Might he have a singleton?

A singleton is almost impossible. He might have preferred it to the spade switch. Also if he has a stiff club, he has a most peculiar shape. He would have to have 2-2-8-1 which might have bid another diamond or 2-3-7-1 which would leave declarer with only three hearts. These boys like to bid a lot, but I don't think their enthusiasm goes so far as to rebid three baggers when there is a good likelihood of getting whacked.

What if partner has two clubs? Can we do anything then?

Yes. I can cash the ace of spades, allowing a club discard, then cash the club ace and give partner a ruff. The diamond return will provide three down.

Is this the best defense?

No. Rather bad in fact.

Why?

If partner has three clubs we will not get a club ruff. Furthermore, unless partner is psychic, he will not ruff the ace of spades and I will not get a diamond lead.

Is it possible to get the best of both worlds? Can I try for a club ruff and still get my trump promotion if there is no club ruff available?

Yes. It can be done. Having won the jack of spades, I cash the ace of clubs. I expect partner to give me count. If I judge partner to have two clubs I will cash the ace of spades and partner will make the obvious club discard. A club ruff and an uppercut will follow.

Is it likely that the required distribution exists?

There is a reasonable chance. For this greedy line to work partner must have 2-2-7-2 shape. This would leave declarer with a four card heart suit. But there are so many high cards missing that declarer could have eight or nine high card points and not feel like selling out to two diamonds. All of this would leave partner with an eleven count, but with, say,

♠ Kx
♡ xx
◇ AKxxxxx
♣ Jx

we would open one diamond and not have any regrets.

At trick four I cash the ace of clubs. This probably is not the card everyone was expecting but no one revokes, declarer playing the queen and partner the four. Noting that the club two is missing, I can conclude that this defense will work. I now cash the spade ace and partner finishes his echo with the two. A club ruff and a diamond return ensue and they are down three.

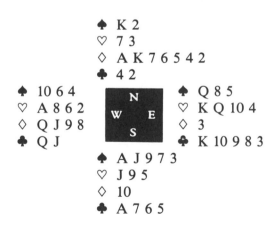

There are quite a few points of interest in this hand. The obvious one is the defense. South was able to combine all his possibilities. Had North played the club two, South would revert to the first plan, leading a suit preference nine of spades for partner to ruff. North would, or should, return a diamond and not try to give South a club ruff.

In the bidding West had a typical competitive decision to make and his two heart bid was normal. I think East went to the well one time too many. After all, he did double one diamond.

Also note the trouble South had in the auction. His system of automatic redoubles with ten points plus led to a guessing game. North-South might have a four spade game available. The trouble is that after redoubling, it is awkward to introduce the spades. I won't comment further here except to say that it seems much better to be able to bid one spade, forcing, over the double.

36

♠ J 9 3
♡ K 10 7
♢ Q 10 8 2
♣ Q 10 5

With no one vul, the auction begins ONE CLUB by LHO, ONE HEART by partner and DOUBLE on my right. This is alerted as a negative double guaranteeing exactly four spades and at least seven points. My values are somewhat tenuous but they do include good trump support so I raise to TWO HEARTS. When LHO bids TWO SPADES, the auction ends.

Dealer: West
Vul: None

WEST	NORTH	EAST	SOUTH
1 ♣	1 ♡	Double*	2 ♡
2 ♠	Pass	Pass	Pass

*Negative
Partner leads the two of spades.

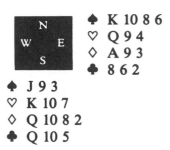

♠ K 10 8 6
♡ Q 9 4
♢ A 9 3
♣ 8 6 2

♠ J 9 3
♡ K 10 7
♢ Q 10 8 2
♣ Q 10 5

Declarer plays off three rounds of trumps ending in dummy. Partner follows a second time and then discards the five of hearts.

What's happening? Are we going to beat this?

At this stage it is reasonable to assume partner has the heart ace for his overcall. He is likely to have a club honor or else he might not have led a trump. Also, I think that in order to beat

119

this, partner will need the king of diamonds. If partner has AJx of clubs, then the jack of diamonds will suffice, but we'll have to get after diamonds right away.

At trick four declarer leads the club deuce from dummy. I start to play the five. But before doing so I reconsider.

Is my first impulse right, or should I play something else?

It seems to me that beating this will require declarer to have only four clubs. If he has five, he will be able to set them up. Even if partner has the AJ doubleton, I don't expect declarer to misguess them.

Why shouldn't he misguess?

Declarer, who is hypothetically missing the ace and king of hearts, will credit me with one of them. Partner would lead a heart with both. Also if partner had the king and queen of diamonds, he might lead one. Plus, my partner is marked with something in clubs by the trump lead. This means that declarer will play me for a high heart honor, a diamond honor, the jack of spades, and consequently, not the ace of clubs.

If I'm going to play declarer for four clubs, I can cater to one possible holding while not giving up the defense should that holding not exist.

What holding is that?

It is AJ9x of clubs.

What can I do?

If I play the five, declarer will play the nine, losing to the king. Later he can hook the jack, scoring three club tricks with the fortunate division. But if I play the queen, declarer will have some problems. If he takes the trick, he will have to go to dummy to lead another club. Since his only entry is a diamond, declarer may be reluctant to do this. Conversely, he may decide to let me hold the trick in which case he will lose two club tricks.

In practice, declarer wins and plays to the ace of diamonds. Next a club and I duck. Declarer gives this quite a bit of thought but eventually does the right thing, playing the nine. Partner takes the king and switches to the heart ace. I cannot afford the ten because declarer might have a stiff. Then another heart lead would establish dummy's queen if declarer finessed the nine. Partner continues with the jack, covered by the queen and king. I switch back to diamonds and we take two more tricks. Making exactly two. I see that declarer did start with the AJ93 of clubs.

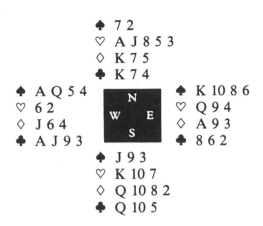

```
              ♠ 7 2
              ♡ A J 8 5 3
              ◇ K 7 5
              ♣ K 7 4
♠ A Q 5 4                      ♠ K 10 8 6
♡ 6 2          N               ♡ Q 9 4
◇ J 6 4      W   E             ◇ A 9 3
♣ A J 9 3      S               ♣ 8 6 2
              ♠ J 9 3
              ♡ K 10 7
              ◇ Q 10 8 2
              ♣ Q 10 5
```

FURTHER ANALYSIS

This turns out to be quite an interesting hand. All of the inferences which were available to South were available to declarer. Declarer was not inclined to play the overcaller for only 10xx of clubs. Not after a trump lead. Further South would more more likely to duck the first club lead with KQx.

One other point of interest is that if declarer did duck the club queen, it would be necessary for the defense to shift diamonds. And not just any diamond.

 A 9 3

Q 10 8 2

South, looking at this layout, has to lead the ten. If declarer has the king it doesn't matter, but if he has the jack, and North the king, the ten is necessary. The play will go,

10-J-K-A.

When North gets in, he will play a diamond and South, with the Q8 over dummy's nine, will get two tricks.

121

In spite of my apparently discouraging seven of hearts, partner could tell I had the king. I would not have a raise without it.

♠ Jxx
♡ 10xx
♦ Qxxx
♣ Q10x

This would not be much of a raise.

It was evident to partner that I could not afford the ten.

Even though it was a hollow victory, we did manage to hold declarer to eight tricks.

37

♠ A 5 3
♡ A K 8 4 3 2
◇ 2
♣ Q 5 3

Everyone is vulnerable and I start things with ONE HEART.
Partner raises to TWO HEARTS and RHO DOUBLES. Who
knows what's right? This hand can produce anything from two
hearts to five hearts. My choices, should I choose to be scien-
tific, are two spades or three clubs. If I decide to be tactical, I
can try three hearts. Or I can apply the bludgeon with four
hearts, and create a guessing game. I choose the latter, bidding
FOUR HEARTS. LHO guesses FOUR SPADES, passed back
to me. Partner may have some idea that his was a forcing pass,
but I don't think so. I pass.

Dealer: South
Vul: Both

SOUTH	WEST	NORTH	EAST
1 ♡	Pass	2 ♡	Double
4 ♡	4 ♠	Pass	Pass
Pass			

Partner's lead is the queen of hearts.

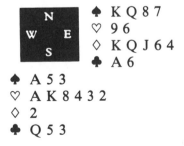

♠ K Q 8 7
♡ 9 6
◇ K Q J 6 4
♣ A 6

♠ A 5 3
♡ A K 8 4 3 2
◇ 2
♣ Q 5 3

There are a number of options. I can overtake and switch to
clubs, hoping partner has the king. Or I can play the two,
expecting partner to switch to clubs, again hoping he has the

123

king. Or I can overtake and switch to my stiff diamond.

Which of these is best?

If partner has the king of clubs, we will need two heart tricks. If partner has the ace of diamonds, it doesn't matter how many hearts we can cash because one diamond ruff will suffice. Since overtaking and returning my diamond will work whenever declarer has two hearts, regardless of other considerations, I will play for a diamond ruff. Win the heart king. Return the two of diamonds, get in with the ace of spades, underlead to partner's jack, diamond ruff. Success.

Is partner likely to have only three hearts? Doesn't his raise tend to show four? Not at all. Even playing four card majors, partner should have no qualms about raising with QJx. Furthermore, if I get lucky and find partner with the ace of diamonds, I won't even need to cash a second heart.

I overtake the queen of hearts with the king and return the diamond two. I don't really expect partner to have the ace and he doesn't. Dummy wins with the jack and, before starting trumps, leads the ace of clubs. This is not what I anticipated. If declarer has the KJx of clubs, he can take a finesse and get rid of dummy's heart. We will lose the communication to get a diamond ruff.

So if declarer has the KJx(x) of clubs we have had it if he has the courage to finesse. Come to think of it, declarer may refuse the finesse and still make four hearts. He can play the ace and king of clubs and then lead the jack. If it is not covered he will discard dummy's heart, giving us a club trick in exchange for a heart trick, but stopping our diamond ruff.

Can we succeed against KJx of clubs, assuming other things are as they appear?

No.

So we have to assume declarer has a different club holding. But whatever it is, why is he leading a club at all?

If he has KJx, he is going to get rid of dummy's heart. But if he has anything else, assuming he has the king, he may still be trying to get rid of dummy's heart.

How?

Say he has K10x. He will play ace, king and ten, losing to my queen, but having rid dummy of that heart. The scissors coup.

Can this be defeated?

Yes. On the second club I can play the queen. If declarer has the dreaded KJx, he makes an overtrick, but then we weren't beating them anyway. But if he doesn't have the jack, then partner will be able to play a high enough club on the third round so that I will not be forced to win the trick.

I choose to play the queen on the second round of clubs, losing to the king as anticipated. Declarer continues with the nine, covered by partner's ten, and declarer, hoping I began with QJx, pitches the heart nine.

When I am able to play low, partner leads a diamond for me to ruff and we have them down one.

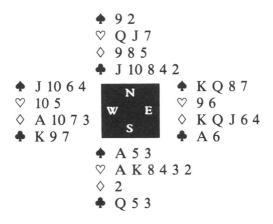

```
               ♠ 9 2
               ♥ Q J 7
               ◊ 9 8 5
               ♣ J 10 8 4 2
♠ J 10 6 4                      ♠ K Q 8 7
♥ 10 5          N               ♥ 9 6
◊ A 10 7 3    W   E             ◊ K Q J 6 4
♣ K 9 7          S              ♣ A 6
               ♠ A 5 3
               ♥ A K 8 4 3 2
               ◊ 2
               ♣ Q 5 3
```

FURTHER ANALYSIS

Declarer's play was well conceived. Note that if South's clubs were QJx, he would have to begin unblocking immediately, dropping the jack on the ace and playing the queen on the next round. This would work if partner had the ten. It would also look a little silly if declarer had K10x and discarded dummy's heart on the ten of clubs. A hard to believe − 650.

North might have played the jack of clubs when declarer played the ace. This would assure South that the queen was a safe play.

Also one of the possible defenses I mentioned was to switch to clubs. It is useful to note that if declarer has any of these distributions, he will still have a club loser, regardless of whether or not I shift to them:

                    ♠ K Q 8 7
                    ♡ 9 6
                    ◇ K Q J 6 4
                    ♣ A 6

♠ J10xx   ♠ Jxxxx   ♠ J10xx
♡ xx   ♡ x   ♡ xx
◇ Axxx   ◇ Axxx   ◇ Ax
♣ xxx   ♣ xxx   ♣ xxxxx

38

♠ K 10 7 3
♡ J 6
◇ 10 9 6 4
♣ A 7 4

We are vulnerable against not and RHO opens ONE CLUB.
I pass and LHO responds ONE HEART. After a ONE NO-
TRUMP rebid by opener, LHO bids TWO HEARTS which
is passed back to me. Even with this minimum, I must give
some thought to reopening. My feelings are that it is a
close decision and I choose to pass only in deference to the
vulnerability.

Dealer:
Vul: North-South

EAST	SOUTH	WEST	NORTH
1 ♣	Pass	1 ♡	Pass
1 NT	Pass	2 ♡	Pass
Pass	Pass		

Partner leads the two of spades and dummy plays the four.

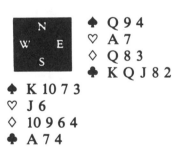

♠ Q 9 4
♡ A 7
◇ Q 8 3
♣ K Q J 8 2

♠ K 10 7 3
♡ J 6
◇ 10 9 6 4
♣ A 7 4

The routine play would be the ten and, unless I can think of a
good reason not to, I will play that card.

Why might I do otherwise?

There are two reasons.

If partner is leading from J8xx, then my proper play would be
the seven, keeping declarer from establishing a second spade
trick.

127

The second reason is that partner might have chosen this moment to underlead the ace of spades. This is not usually done, but on rare occasions it is right, so I will consider the possibility. If I judge that partner has done this, I must rise with the king.

What information do I already have?

Partner did not lead a diamond, so he doesn't have the ace-king. Whatever he has in spades, the ace and king of diamonds would be a more attractive choice.

Declarer also has either the ace or jack of spades and he has a six card heart suit. If he has only a five card suit, it will be a good one which would suggest no ace of spades.

I'm not sure yet about whether the king is right, but for the moment, I'm going to reject the seven. The club suit is likely to provide declarer with tricks so I'm not going to worry about giving him a second spade trick. I'm going to make whatever play I judge necessary to get us the maximum number of spade tricks.

It gets more and more confusing. What if partner is leading from a three card suit? If he has led from J8x, then the seven is the winning play.

What can I say? It's hands like this that drives defenders crazy. If we were playing third and fifth (third best from an even number and low from an odd number) then I would know that partner's two showed three. But we aren't playing that and my problems remain.

There are two reasons for my playing the king and I believe they may add up sufficiently to motivate me.

First declarer might go up with the queen if he had the ace. If he had two spades (Ax) he would certainly do that. And if he had three spades he might consider it.

Secondly, this is one of those sequences where partner might actually underlead an ace. From his point of view the dummy rates to have some spade strength and declarer rates to be weak. Also, dummy ought to have no more than three spades and declarer is unlikely to have a stiff, since then I would have five spades and would likely have reopened with two spades.

Come to think of it there is one more reason to play the king. If it wins then it is almost guaranteed that partner has the ace of diamonds rather than the king. This is because partner would be less likely to underlead an ace if there were a reasonable alternative.

Is there any danger that the king play will find declarer with AJ doubleton?

No. This one danger I need not worry about. That would leave partner with 8652 and we do not lead the two from such worthless holdings.

The king it is. Winning.

And now?

This is the easy part. I already expect partner to have the ace of diamonds and since things are going well, I can hope he has the jack also. I return the ten to declarer's two, partner's seven and dummy's queen. Dummy leads the club king and I take it immediately, partner giving count with the three. I return the four of diamonds and partner cashes two more diamond tricks and the ace of spades. Eventually he scores the queen of hearts as well and declarer comes up one trick short.

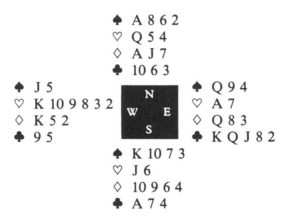

```
              ♠ A 8 6 2
              ♡ Q 5 4
              ◇ A J 7
              ♣ 10 6 3
♠ J 5                        ♠ Q 9 4
♡ K 10 9 8 3 2    N         ♡ A 7
◇ K 5 2        W     E       ◇ Q 8 3
♣ 9 5             S          ♣ K Q J 8 2
              ♠ K 10 7 3
              ♡ J 6
              ◇ 10 9 6 4
              ♣ A 7 4
```

This is a quite complex hand and while the play of the spade king was well-reasoned, it need not have been right. Who knows, for instance, how often partner would lead from the J82 of spades? This is certainly possible and then the play of the seven would be the winner.

FURTHER ANALYSIS

Declarer could, on the actual hand, have played dummy's nine. That might cause South to play the ten. But then declarer could hardly appreciate the problem that South had and might not have anticipated the consequences of playing low.

39

♠ 10 8 6 4
♡ 9 8 3
◊ Q 4 2
♣ K Q 2

No one is vul and partner opens ONE HEART. I respond
TWO HEARTS although I'm not too proud of it. A very
reasonable alternative of one notrump could easily work out
better. The one thing I'm not going to do is respond one spade.

LHO comes in with THREE DIAMONDS and that ends the
auction.

Dealer: North
Vul: None

NORTH	EAST	SOUTH	WEST
1 ♡	Pass	2 ♡	3 ◊
Pass	Pass	Pass	

Partner leads the king of spades and a very reasonable
dummy appears. I hope partner is not leading from the KQ.

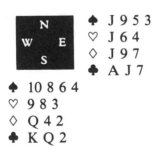

♠ J 9 5 3
♡ J 6 4
◊ J 9 7
♣ A J 7

♠ 10 8 6 4
♡ 9 8 3
◊ Q 4 2
♣ K Q 2

I cannot do anything except play the four. The worst happens
as declarer takes the ace. Now come the ace and king of
diamonds, partner following once and then discarding the heart
seven.

Rightly or wrongly, I give count by playing the four and two.
Someday perhaps I will lose a trick by this, but I have found
most declarers to be untrusting sorts. They don't believe me. Of

more importance, partner gets a count and he will not wonder if I have Qxx or Qxxx should he even think that I have the queen.

Declarer now leads the seven of spades and partner rises with the queen.

What's happening?

By now the hand is an open book. Partner has the KQ(x) of spades, a stiff diamond, nothing in clubs and the AQxxx of hearts.

Why not six hearts?

Because he would compete to three hearts with six of them plus a stiff diamond.

Why exactly the AQ of hearts?

Because with better hearts he would lead one in preference to the spade. For example:

♠ KQx
♡ AKxxx
♢ x
♣ xxxx

And with less than the AQ he would not have an opening bid.

What is the black suit distribution?

I'm inclined to give him three spades and four clubs. With five-five he might have competed with three hearts. This isn't all that clear because the three diamond bid has taken away our game tries. Three hearts over three diamonds is not quite as competitive as it would be had they overcalled with three clubs instead.

With all of this information is there anything we can do to help the defense? In fact, is there a defense?

Yes. There is defense. If partner can be restrained from laying down the ace of hearts, declarer will come to five diamonds, two spades and one club. The trick is to keep partner from trying to cash out.

How do we do this?

Play the six of spades on partner's queen. Whatever he makes of it, he should assume that I do not have the king of hearts. If I did have it, I would play as high a spade as I could afford to get partner to cash out. When I am not able to give him a suit preference for hearts, he should work out that I want a club shift. He should not feel that the six of spades is asking for a club. He should feel that it is denying interest in hearts. On this hand he can work out that I want a club because there is nothing left that I can have for my raise.

Partner appears to have interpreted my intentions correctly because he shifts to a club. Declarer wins and cashes the jack of spades, hoping for the ten to drop. It doesn't and he goes one down.

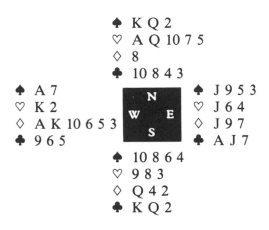

♠ K Q 2
♡ A Q 10 7 5
◇ 8
♣ 10 8 4 3

♠ A 7
♡ K 2
◇ A K 10 6 5 3
♣ 9 6 5

♠ J 9 5 3
♡ J 6 4
◇ J 9 7
♣ A J 7

♠ 10 8 6 4
♡ 9 8 3
◇ Q 4 2
♣ K Q 2

FURTHER ANALYSIS

Even if declarer had held three spades, this defense would have held him to the minimum number of tricks.

Note that if South's spades had been 1084, then there might have been some confusion when he played the eight on the second round. North would have to guess whether South had 864 and was asking for a heart or 1084 and was denying interest in hearts. Fortunately most of your messages will not be ambiguous.

The exercise of reconstructing the hands is an extremely important one. Note the inferences available and how they led to an almost double dummy conclusion. Of additional importance is that you know partner's tendencies and how he will act in certain situations. For instance, my current partner could be counted on to bid three hearts with:

♠ KQ
♡ AQ10xxx
◇ x
♣ 10xxx

What would your partner do in a similar situation? The better you know your partner, the better you will be able to judge what he has and your inferences will be all the better for it.

40

♠ K 3
♡ K 9 4 3 2
◇ K 8
♣ J 8 7 6

We are not vul against vulnerable opponents. RHO opens
ONE DIAMOND and I compete with ONE HEART. LHO bids
ONE SPADE and opener alerts that this shows five. With four
they would make a negative double. Opener rebids TWO DIA-
MONDS and is raised to THREE DIAMONDS. Opener still
has some reserves and tries THREE NOTRUMP.

Dealer: East
Vul: East-West

EAST	SOUTH	WEST	NORTH
1 ◇	1 ♡	1 ♠	Pass
2 ◇	Pass	3 ◇	Pass
3 NT	Pass	Pass	Pass

I don't think we are going to beat this but I do have to lead. I
lead the heart three.

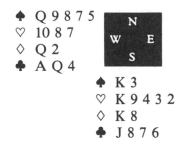

♠ Q 9 8 7 5
♡ 10 8 7
◇ Q 2
♣ A Q 4

♠ K 3
♡ K 9 4 3 2
◇ K 8
♣ J 8 7 6

Dummy's choice of three diamonds looks at first to be a bit
of an overbid, but it seems like too good a hand to pass. Three
diamonds looks like a practical choice. In the meantime my
heart lead goes to partner's queen and declarer's ace. Declarer
leads the club nine to the ace and partner's two, and tries the
queen of diamonds. Partner follows with the three, declarer the

four and I grab the trick.

What now? What are my choices?

I can try to set up the hearts, hoping my king of spades is an entry.

I can continue clubs.

I can lead the king of spades hoping for partner to have the AJ.

What is known?

Declarer has the AJ(x) of hearts and probably six diamonds to the AJ. Also he will have the spade ace or the club king, but not both of them. If he had both, the two diamond rebid would have been a serious underbid.

Does declarer have two or three hearts?

Probably three. If my partner had Qxx plus either the spade ace or the club king, he might have raised.

What black honor does declarer have?

Probably the king of clubs. Without it he would have either finessed the queen or attacked diamonds from his hand rather than risk setting up the club suit for the defense.

If declarer has the club king will he have enough tricks?

Oh yes. He will have a heart, five diamonds, three clubs and, if I give it to him, an extra heart trick as well.

What is declarer's shape?

From the play in clubs and diamonds, it looks like declarer has six diamonds and three clubs. From partner's failure to raise hearts I can conclude declarer has three hearts and possibly even four.

And the best defense?

Since declarer will have enough tricks if he can get at them, I switch to the king of spades. Partner plays the six and declarer the jack. This means declarer is 1-3-6-3. It may be insulting to partner but I cash the heart king before leading my second spade. This provides us with three spades, a heart and a diamond. Maybe there's something to this longest and strongest after all?

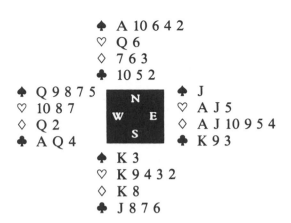

```
              ♠ A 10 6 4 2
              ♡ Q 6
              ◇ 7 6 3
              ♣ 10 5 2
♠ Q 9 8 7 5                      ♠ J
♡ 10 8 7        N               ♡ A J 5
◇ Q 2        W     E            ◇ A J 10 9 5 4
♣ A Q 4         S               ♣ K 9 3
              ♠ K 3
              ♡ K 9 4 3 2
              ◇ K 8
              ♣ J 8 7 6
```

Declarer might have played diamonds from his hand even with the actual hand. Had I won the king, it would have been a bit more difficult to switch to the king of spades. Also, if the king of diamonds were onside, that would tend to confirm the ace and king of spades were in my hand. After all, would I overcall with, say,

$$
\begin{aligned}
&♠ \ \text{Axx} \\
&♡ \ \text{K9xxx} \\
&◇ \ \text{xx} \\
&♣ \ \text{Jxx}
\end{aligned}
$$

This would be a little light. In any event, declarer's line was not hopeless. It would have succeeded legitimately 75% of the time and also when the defense erred.

41

♠ K 2
♡ J 10 7 6
◇ J 9
♣ K 9 8 6 5

No one is vul and the auction starts on my left with pass. Partner and I pass throughout and I end up on lead against four spades.

Dealer: West
Vul: None

WEST	NORTH	EAST	SOUTH
Pass	Pass	1 ◇	Pass
1 ♡	Pass	1 ♠	Pass
2 ♠	Pass	4 ♠	Pass
Pass	Pass		

I have no reason not to lead my fourth best club and I am not unhappy to do so.

♠ Q 9 7 6
♡ A 8 5 4
◇ 10 6 3
♣ Q 2

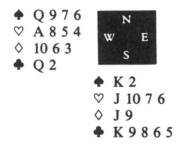

♠ K 2
♡ J 10 7 6
◇ J 9
♣ K 9 8 6 5

My club six goes to partner's ace and he returns the club three. Declarer follows with the four and the jack. It looks like partner has four clubs to the ace-ten.

At trick three I switch to the heart six. Declarer wins partner's queen with the king and leads the three of spades towards dummy's queen.

What's the big idea?

From the auction it is clear that declarer has the ace of spades.

How many spades does he have?

Almost certainly he has four. He is either 4-1-6-2 or 4-2-5-2. Conceivably he is 4-1-4-4, but if so, he has found a curious false card at trick two.

Who has the jack of spades?

It is very unlikely that declarer has it. If he had it he would have arranged to lead from dummy in order to take a finesse. He could do this by winning the ace of hearts.

Alternatively he could lay down the ace, catering to the stiff king in either hand.

What is the verdict?

It is simply this. Declarer is missing the jack of spades and is in the process of drawing and guessing trump.

Should I grab the king?

No. Declarer has one of the following trump combinations:

Q976	Q976
A10xx	Axxx

With the second of these combinations he would tend to play ace and another. But with the first combination he would try to combine his chances. With only one entry to dummy, he would win the heart in hand and lead towards the queen. He would guess to play the nine or the queen and, if he misguessed, would reenter dummy with the heart ace and take a finesse through RHO for the remaining honor.

What does this mean?

What it means is that I have to duck this spade and, furthermore, I have to do it smoothly. I can't afford to cogitate and give the show away. I play the two.

Apparently I have either failed to duck smoothly enough or declarer is just a good guesser because he plays the queen. A spade to his ace and he claims, losing one additional trick to partner's trump jack.

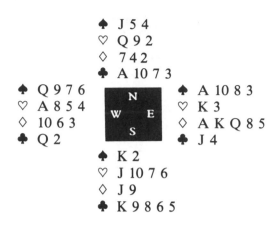

```
                    ♠ J 5 4
                    ♡ Q 9 2
                    ◇ 7 4 2
                    ♣ A 10 7 3
   ♠ Q 9 7 6        ┌─────────┐    ♠ A 10 8 3
   ♡ A 8 5 4        │    N    │    ♡ K 3
   ◇ 10 6 3         │ W     E │    ◇ A K Q 8 5
   ♣ Q 2            │    S    │    ♣ J 4
                    └─────────┘
                    ♠ K 2
                    ♡ J 10 7 6
                    ◇ J 9
                    ♣ K 9 8 6 5
```

The problem of this hand is a fairly simple one. Once you realize that declarer cannot really have the AJxx of trumps, it is proper to duck. The important thing is to recognize the situation in time to make your play unconcerned and in tempo. On this hand the worst happened. Declarer guessed the suit, but we still got a trick. Even if the bidding had been

1 ♠	Pass	2 ♠	Pass
4 ♠	Pass	Pass	Pass

and the defense went the same way, it would be sound play for you to duck when declarer leads the three of spades. Even if you suspect he has a five card suit, you should duck. Any declarer who starts the spades in this fashion will play the nine from dummy. And he may finesse later into your king. This interesting sequence of plays would turn a one loser suit into a potential no loser suit and then into a potential two loser suit.

Wonderful game, this bridge.

42

♠ A Q 4 2
♡ Q J 7 2
◇ Q 2
♣ A 5 3

Vul versus not, I hold a rather good hand and am considering whether to open one notrump. I don't get the chance because LHO opens ONE NOTRUMP in first seat. RHO jumps to THREE SPADES and opener raises to FOUR SPADES. Just like I'm not even here. Their card says 15-17 but it doesn't make much difference. Whatever their range, they are going to have most of the high cards.

Dealer: West
Vul: North-South

WEST	NORTH	EAST	SOUTH
1 NT	Pass	3 ♠	Pass
4 ♠	Pass	Pass	Pass

What should I lead? This does not look like the time to lead the queen of diamonds, and the situation is hardly serious enough to underlead the ace of clubs. With my long spades, I feel that if I can get my heart suit going I may be able to tap declarer. Perhaps I can set up a long spade.

Which heart should I lead?

On this hand I am going to lead the two. The reason for leading the queen would be that I hope to trap the king in dummy. But my partner isn't going to have the ace of hearts on this sequence. But he may have the ten.

I lead the heart two and see that partner does not even have the ten.

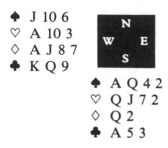

♠ J 10 6
♡ A 10 3
◇ A J 8 7
♣ K Q 9

♠ A Q 4 2
♡ Q J 7 2
◇ Q 2
♣ A 5 3

We get lucky. Dummy plays the three, partner the nine and declarer the king. This sequence of plays marks declarer with the eight. His play was correct, but I think we may make him pay for it.

At trick two declarer leads the ten of clubs.

Should I take it?

Yes. If declarer has a stiff club, I may be setting up an extra trick for him, but this time I know where we will get it back. I continue with the queen of hearts, taken by dummy's ace. Partner plays the four and declarer the eight. When declarer finesses the jack of spades into me, partner follows and I win. I could duck this if I wished.

When I play the heart jack, declarer looks annoyed, but still manages to ruff it. Now he leads the king of spades.

Should I take this?

No. I intend to establish trump control. My plan is to take the next spade and then tap declarer out of his remaining trump. If I take this round of spades declarer will be able to ruff the fourth round of hearts in dummy, and then draw trump. I must duck this spade and take the next so that my tapping game will have some teeth to it. This is successful and eventually we come to one club and three spades.

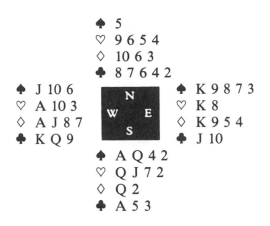

The defense here was rather interesting. First came the conclusion that partner could not hold a high card, hence the underlead of the QJ72. On this hand South got lucky. But there are some other combinations where it might work. Here are a few of them:

	AK3	Declarer might judge to take the king. Especially if he has an immediate discard available.
QJ72		
	1054	

	AK10	Likewise.
QJ72		
	543	

	A86	Declarer might wish to be in dummy.
QJ72		
	K10	

Second, it was necessary for South to take the club at once. This exception to the general rule that you should duck in this situation occurs because there is a known effective defense available.

And third, the defense had to hold up in trump so that the final heart lead would attack the long trump holding rather than the short trumps.

43

♠ A Q 2
♡ K 10 6 4
♢ 9 5 3
♣ 10 5 4

No one is vul and RHO opens ONE DIAMOND. I pass and when LHO responds ONE SPADE, opener raises to TWO SPADES. Responder offers a choice with THREE NOTRUMP, but opener converts back to FOUR SPADES.

Dealer: East
Vul: None

EAST	SOUTH	WEST	NORTH
1 ♢	Pass	1 ♠	Pass
2 ♠	Pass	3 NT	Pass
4 ♠	Pass	Pass	Pass

Partner gets off to the queen of clubs which goes to declarer's ace.

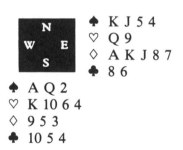

♠ K J 5 4
♡ Q 9
♢ A K J 8 7
♣ 8 6

♠ A Q 2
♡ K 10 6 4
♢ 9 5 3
♣ 10 5 4

What's up?
If declarer's bidding is to be believed, he is going to make four spades rather easily. He can hardly have less than

♠ xxxx
♡ Axx
♢ Qxx
♣ AKx.

It is possible that he has the jack of hearts and no queen of diamonds, but even so it's going to be uphill to beat this.

At trick two, declarer leads the ten of spades which rides to me. What should I do?

This hand is almost surely iron clad. As far as I can tell, the only possible defense would be to play partner for a diamond void plus the jack of hearts. Or perhaps I should play partner for the ace of hearts and play declarer for being a wild optimist.

Which is it?

I can't really see either of these working. I actually think we are playing for overtricks, or maybe some ego points.

Come to think of it, it's going to be hard to stop even an overtrick. Hearts look like our best bet, but when I win the queen of spades, I won't be able to lead a heart from my side. And if we can't set up a heart trick immediately, we won't get it because declarer will be able to pitch his heart losers on dummy's diamonds.

Is this a certainty?

No. But it is likely. If declarer has, say, 4-3-4-2 distribution, then he will not be able to pitch all his hearts.

Is this shape likely?

No. It leaves my partner with a stiff diamond. I think that with the bad hand he is known to hold, he would have led it.

Are there any other distributions which won't permit the hearts to get away?

Yes. 4-4-3-2.

Is this a likely shape?

No. With this shape, declarer would respond one heart rather than one spade.

Therefore, barring declarer having some most peculiar hand, he will have little trouble making five.

Is there any way to manufacture a trick given we don't have it legitimately?

Perhaps. Winning the spade lead with the ace rather than the queen, and then returning a heart, may convince declarer he doesn't have to take the heart finesse. He will have available the line of winning the ace of hearts, drawing trumps via another "finesse" and claiming.

This is a realistic chance and I decide to give it a try. The effect is quite satisfying. I win the ace of spades and return the four of hearts. Declarer gives little thought to it and goes up with the ace. When I score the spade queen, declarer is mildly miffed and when I cash the heart king, he is distinctly aggravated. It's only a trick, but, for sure, it's more satisfying than most.

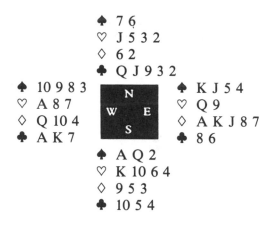

	♠ 7 6	
	♡ J 5 3 2	
	◇ 6 2	
	♣ Q J 9 3 2	
♠ 10 9 8 3		♠ K J 5 4
♡ A 8 7		♡ Q 9
◇ Q 10 4		◇ A K J 8 7
♣ A K 7		♣ 8 6
	♠ A Q 2	
	♡ K 10 6 4	
	◇ 9 5 3	
	♣ 10 5 4	

FURTHER ANALYSIS

Note that South could have defended in the same fashion with AQ alone as opposed to the actual AQx. Only if declarer had a six bagger would he fail to take the finesse again. This defensive play is usually quite safe.

Of minor interest is that this defense also takes advantage of that rare situation where partner does somehow have the ace of hearts. It would not be a good result to play, say, three rounds of spades and then have declarer concede a heart trick at trick thirteen. As I said, this is a practical impossibility.

44

♠ ——
♡ K Q J 10 7 6 3
◇ A 10 5 3
♣ A 8

Vul vs not, I pick up the best hand I've held in quite a while. It is distinctly disappointing to hear partner pass and RHO open FOUR SPADES. Anything could be right but aside from five, or perhaps six, hearts, nothing seems sensible. I choose FIVE HEARTS, fully prepared to go for five hundred or to miss a slam.

It seems I needn't have worried about going for a number because LHO jumps to SIX SPADES. It's hard to believe he expects to make this. It must be a sacrifice. Partner DOUBLES and RHO passes. It is tempting to play partner for some specific cards and bid again but I reject this as fantasy.

Dealer: North
Vul: North-South

NORTH	EAST	SOUTH	WEST
Pass	4 ♠	5 ♡	6 ♠
Double	Pass	Pass	Pass

I lead the heart king.

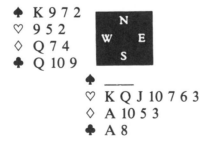

♠ K 9 7 2
♡ 9 5 2
◇ Q 7 4
♣ Q 10 9

♠ ——
♡ K Q J 10 7 6 3
◇ A 10 5 3
♣ A 8

Certainly the dummy has nothing to write home about. From his point of view we could make a grand. Perhaps we can.

No. Partner plays the heart eight and declarer wins the ace. So much for our grand. Declarer draws three rounds of trump, partner following with the six, four and eight. Next he plays the club two towards dummy's Q109. I duck and the queen wins. The ten of clubs is now led to my ace, partner so far contributing the three and five.

What's going on?

I know that declarer has six spades AQJ10, the heart ace, and some number of clubs to the king. If declarer has six clubs, then he is going to make his contract.

What if he has less than six clubs? Is there any danger?

Yes. In fact this hand is getting a little bit nervous. Since declarer hasn't claimed, I assume he isn't six-six in the blacks, but if he is six-five, then we have a red suit trick coming. Do I need to guess what to do? Does it matter?

Yes. It does matter.

Is it just a guess? How can I tell whether declarer or partner has the missing four of hearts?

It doesn't matter who has it. The key is that if declarer has five clubs, he will to get two discards from dummy. He can get rid of both remaining hearts or two of the three diamonds. It is therefore right to lead the queen of hearts. If it is ruffed, you will still get at least one diamond. If, however, you lead the ace of diamonds and *it* gets ruffed, declarer may be able to pitch both hearts from dummy and then ruff his last heart.

In practice, the heart queen wins. The actual distribution was the one I had to worry about.

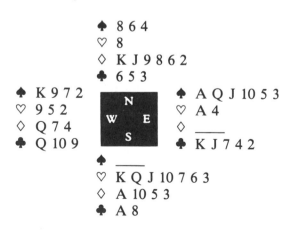

RHO is busy berating his partner for bidding six spades. I wonder what he would be saying if I had been in six hearts making with a spade lead.

FURTHER ANALYSIS

It is easy for South to make a careless play of the diamond ace at trick seven. Dummy's distribution was the key to this problem. Had dummy had one more spade and one less diamond, there would be no solution.

45

♠ 6 5
♡ 10 7 6 3
♢ Q J 4
♣ A K J 3

With no one vul, my RHO opens TWO DIAMONDS. I pass and LHO leaps to FOUR SPADES, ending the auction.

Dealer: East
Vul: None

EAST	SOUTH	WEST	NORTH
2 ♢	Pass	4 ♠	Pass
Pass	Pass		

I assume two diamonds was weak. My partner doesn't care or is sure he knows. He leads the king of hearts.

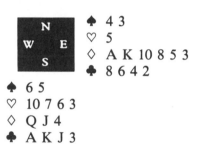

♠ 4 3
♡ 5
♢ A K 10 8 5 3
♣ 8 6 4 2

♠ 6 5
♡ 10 7 6 3
♢ Q J 4
♣ A K J 3

I play the three and partner shifts to the five of clubs. My king wins as declarer follows with the ten. It could be right to continue clubs, but since I have the diamond suit stopped, I switch to a trump. Declarer wins the ace and plays a diamond to the nine, dummy's ten and my jack. Now I have a number of options. I can continue with my second trump or I can attempt to cash another club trick.

Is one of these better?
Very likely.
What is best?

Almost certainly the best play is to return a diamond. Declarer appears to have a weakish hand with six or seven solid spades and not much else. Based on his line of play, I suspect he has six spades. With seven, he could ruff a heart and take seven spades, one heart and two diamonds. His actual line of play would be silly if he had seven spades because the defense could return a second trump and declarer would be at the mercy of a diamond break.

As the hand is being played, declarer will succeed if the queen and jack of diamonds are onside or if the defense fails to return a diamond. True, a diamond return permits declarer to get his heart ruff in dummy. But if it was all that important, then he would have taken it earlier.

I expect declarer has almost exactly

♠ AKQxxx
♡ xxxx
◇ xx
♣ x

I'm going to return a diamond which will forever cut declarer off from his suit. I'll know soon enough if this is right.

It is. Declarer now has only eight tricks and goes down two. He could have held it to down one.

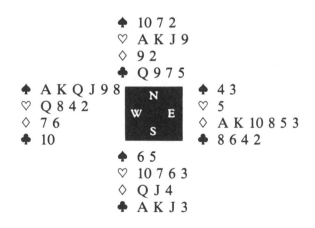

```
              ♠ 10 7 2
              ♡ A K J 9
              ◇ 9 2
              ♣ Q 9 7 5
♠ A K Q J 9 8          ♠ 4 3
♡ Q 8 4 2      N       ♡ 5
◇ 7 6       W     E    ◇ A K 10 8 5 3
♣ 10           S       ♣ 8 6 4 2
              ♠ 6 5
              ♡ 10 7 6 3
              ◇ Q J 4
              ♣ A K J 3
```

FURTHER ANALYSIS

When declarer makes a funny looking play such as finessing the ten of diamonds before drawing trump, it is usually symptomatic of the sort of problem he actually had on this hand. That is, he could not draw trumps first because that would leave him with a number of heart losers. Since the trump switch meant that he could not ruff enough heart losers, he tried the diamond suit hoping for a fortunate lie of the cards or a defensive error.

46

♠ 10 9 8 5
♡ Q 6 5
◇ K 5 4
♣ Q J 9

My vulnerable RHO opens ONE CLUB and this is alerted as forcing with sixteen or more high card points. I love to get in there after a forcing club, but one of the prerequisites is a suit of some sort. I don't have one and, since I don't care much for psyches, I pass. LHO responds ONE HEART, also alerted. It is semi-positive and does not show anything in hearts. Partner passes and opener rebids ONE SPADE. No alerts. LHO Bids ONE NOTRUMP and opener rebids TWO HEARTS. This is raised to FOUR HEARTS and there is another alert. This, it seems, is a minimum semi-positive. With a maximum responder would raise to three hearts—game forcing, leaving room for cue bidding.

Dealer: East
Vul: East-West

EAST	SOUTH	WEST	NORTH
1 ♣	Pass	1 ♡	Pass
1 ♠	Pass	1 NT	Pass
2 ♡	Pass	4 ♡	Pass
Pass	Pass		

I reach for the club queen, but am informed it is not my lead. I had forgotten about the one heart bid. It is partner's lead and he chooses the three of clubs. This is a good sign. If we both want to lead clubs the odds are that one of us is right.

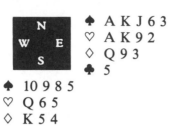

	♠ A K J 6 3
	♡ A K 9 2
	◇ Q 9 3
	♣ 5

♠ 10 9 8 5
♡ Q 6 5
◇ K 5 4
♣ Q J 9

My jack is taken by the ace. Declarer plays the ace and king of spades, felling partner's doubleton queen and ruffs a spade with the jack. Partner plays the club deuce. Next come the ace and king of hearts, partner following twice with small ones. Dummy's jack of spades is cashed, declarer discarding the six of diamonds, and partner the seven of diamonds. When the thirteenth spade is led I have my first decision. Should I ruff?

No. If I ruff in, declarer will have ten tricks. The seven already in, two more trumps and a diamond ruff in his hand. Instead I discard the five of diamonds and partner the seven of clubs.

What is the defensive plan there?

It is quite simple. I hope to get in and draw an additional round of trump.

Do I have an entry to do this?

Probably. For two reasons it looks like partner has the ace of diamonds. One, partner signalled with the seven, and, two, declarer's bidding showed a weakish hand. He ought not to have two aces. Anyway, we won't beat it if declarer has the ace of diamonds. For that reason alone I will credit partner with it.

When dummy leads the three of diamonds I check what I know. For instance, is there any chance that declarer will ruff this?

Declarer is known to have two spades, four hearts and four clubs. This club distribution is known because partner led the three and discarded the two. Hence he started with five of them.

All of this leaves declarer with 2-4-3-4. Guaranteed.

I do rise with the king of diamonds, felling declarer's jack, and draw another round of trump. My club return forces dummy to ruff and partner has the last two tricks.

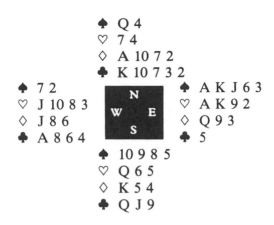

```
                    ♠ Q 4
                    ♡ 7 4
                    ◊ A 10 7 2
                    ♣ K 10 7 3 2
    ♠ 7 2                        ♠ A K J 6 3
    ♡ J 10 8 3         N         ♡ A K 9 2
    ◊ J 8 6        W      E      ◊ Q 9 3
    ♣ A 8 6 4         S          ♣ 5
                    ♠ 10 9 8 5
                    ♡ Q 6 5
                    ◊ K 5 4
                    ♣ Q J 9
```

FURTHER ANALYSIS

In the end game if South ducks the diamond, North will be end-played. A club will permit a crossruff and a diamond will set up a diamond trick if declarer puts in the nine.

Declarer could have made four hearts in a variety of ways, but his actual line would be taken by many declarers. As it went, South had two opportunities to err. Not ruffing the spade was easy enough. It is often right not to ruff when you can expect to get in later and draw two trumps for one.

Rising with the king of diamonds was a good play. Of note here is that even if you could not tell that partner had the ace of diamonds, it would still be right to defend as described. Once again, if declarer has the ace of diamonds, four hearts is unbeatable. It was not difficult to play the king of diamonds on this hand because the bidding and the play both suggested it would win. But sometimes you don't have certainties and you have to make assumptions.

47

♠ J 7 3
♡ 7 4
◇ K Q 3 2
♣ J 9 4 2

No one is vul and partner opens ONE CLUB. RHO overcalls TWO NOTRUMP which is alerted as showing the red suits. The only bid I might consider is three clubs. But since I have a minimum hand, don't want a club lead, and have most of my values in their suits, I pass. LHO bids THREE CLUBS. RHO answers THREE HEARTS and is raised to FOUR HEARTS.

Dealer: North
Vul: None

NORTH	EAST	SOUTH	WEST
1 ♣	2 NT	Pass	3 ♣
Pass	3 ♡	Pass	4 ♡
Pass	Pass	Pass	

Before I lead I ask what three clubs was. It was asking for a five card heart suit.

In spite of partner not having doubled three clubs I lead the two. Dummy is a little surprising.

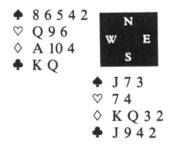

♠ 8 6 5 4 2
♡ Q 9 6
◇ A 10 4
♣ K Q

♠ J 7 3
♡ 7 4
◇ K Q 3 2
♣ J 9 4 2

Partner takes the first trick with the ace and leads back the king and ace of spades. Declarer plays the nine and ruffs the second with the trump two.

What is declarer's shape?

It's most likely to be five-five. He has shown one spade. The auction says five hearts. Assuming he hasn't four diamonds to the jack, the question is whether he has five or six diamonds. If he has six, that would leave partner with 4-3-0-6. I think he would have done something over three clubs with that, so I am pretty sure declarer is 1-5-5-2.

Before touching trump, declarer leads the diamond five. When I duck, dummy wins the ten. Now come three rounds of trump: a heart to declarer's ace, back to the queen, and to declarer's king. Partner shows up with the 1053.

Declarer leads the diamond jack.

Ought I to cover or not?

No. Declarer can win this, and then win the ace, but I will still have a diamond stopper. Declarer will need two entries to his hand to set up his long diamond and then to enjoy it. Since he has only one entry, his last trump, he will be unable to win a long diamond, and will be down one.

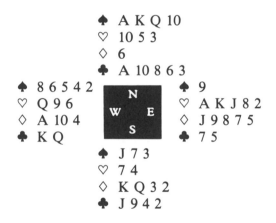

```
                ♠  A K Q 10
                ♡  10 5 3
                ◇  6
                ♣  A 10 8 6 3
    ♠ 8 6 5 4 2                    ♠ 9
    ♡ Q 9 6          N             ♡ A K J 8 2
    ◇ A 10 4     W       E         ◇ J 9 8 7 5
    ♣ K Q           S             ♣ 7 5
                ♠  J 7 3
                ♡  7 4
                ◇  K Q 3 2
                ♣  J 9 4 2
```

FURTHER ANALYSIS

As long as South does not release his diamond stopper prematurely, declarer will fall one short.

I don't care much for East's bidding. The final contract was OK, but the method used to reach it was somewhat poor. When you have two suits of such different quality, you should use a two suited convention when the lower of the two is the better suit. That way responder, with no preference between the two suits, can always bid the lower one knowing that this must be as good a contract as is available. With this hand, East would be better placed to overcall one heart. With the red suits reversed, the two notrump call would be more reasonable.

48

♠ 10 8 7 2
♡ Q 10 7
◇ 9 8 2
♣ 9 3 2

Vul versus not, I hold one of my lesser hands of recent days.
It improves slightly when partner opens ONE SPADE. RHO
DOUBLES and I pass. When LHO bids TWO DIAMONDS,
partner DOUBLES and RHO raises to THREE DIAMONDS. I
consider three spades but, feeling cowardly today, I pass. Three
diamonds is passed out.

Dealer: North
Vul: North-South

NORTH	EAST	SOUTH	WEST
1 ♠	Double	Pass	2 ◇
Double	3 ◇	Pass	Pass
Pass			

Partner leads the king of spades.

♠ J 5
♡ K 9 4 3
◇ A K Q
♣ K J 8 4

♠ 10 8 7 2
♡ Q 10 7
◇ 9 8 2
♣ 9 3 2

How should I defend?
With such a bad hand, it does not seem likely that I can play a
constructive part in the defense, but I think there is something I
can do here.
And that is?
What I would like to do is somehow to get partner to shift to

a heart. There is a good chance that partner is 5-3-2-3 and, if so, a heart shift will be more effective than a club.

What does partner have?

I would judge him to have something along the lines of:

♠ AKxxx		♠ AKQxx		♠ KQxxx
♡ Axx	or	♡ Axx	or	♡ AJx
◇ xx		◇ xx		◇ xx
♣ Axx		♣ Qxx		♣ AQx

If partner has the first hand, the defense matters. If he has the second hand, nothing matters. If he has the third hand, declarer will succeed if he guesses at all well.

How can I get partner to do the right thing?

The one thing which is clear cut is that I can do nothing at trick one to direct a specific shift. I can play the two, which will tell partner I don't like spades, but it will carry no message as to whether I prefer hearts or clubs, or even have a preference. I can play a higher spade than the two, but if I do this, I must not give a high-low. Partner will construe that as showing a doubleton and may give a sluff-ruff.

Is there a way to request a heart shift?

Yes. I can play the seven or eight of spades and when partner continues with the ace, assuming he has it, I will drop the ten.

It remains to be seen whether partner has the ace-king and then whether or not we are on the same wave length. I follow with the eight. Partner continues with the ace and I drop the ten. Partner looks at this for a while and switches to the heart ace. I encourage and partner continues. This leads to down one.

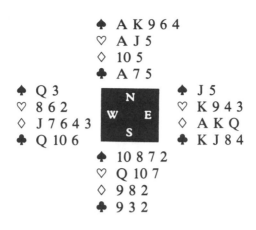

```
              ♠ A K 9 6 4
              ♡ A J 5
              ◇ 10 5
              ♣ A 7 5
   ♠ Q 3          N          ♠ J 5
   ♡ 8 6 2      W     E      ♡ K 9 4 3
   ◇ J 7 6 4 3     S         ◇ A K Q
   ♣ Q 10 6                  ♣ K J 8 4
              ♠ 10 8 7 2
              ♡ Q 10 7
              ◇ 9 8 2
              ♣ 9 3 2
```

FURTHER ANALYSIS

Some players take the view that signalling as I did does not re-quest a heart switch. They play that it denies the ability to stand a switch. If they wanted a switch to either hearts or clubs, they would play the two and then hope partner could work it out. There is some merit to this. On this hand I can insist on a heart switch but I cannot insist on a club switch. I cannot play in any manner to specifically deny interest in a shift.

Compare:

My Way		Their Way	
7-10	lead hearts	7-10	can't stand anything
7-2	lead spades	7-2	lead spades
2-7	you figure it out	2-7	you figure it out, but I do prefer something. More likely clubs than hearts.
2-10	Probably does not exist although perhaps since 7-10 equals hearts, then 2-10 equals clubs.	2-10	Hearts. But note that partner may not cash the ace to find out what's happening. He may try to guess at trick two.

161

To bid three spades over three diamonds would not be outlandish. I did pass after the takeout double, so I can't really have very much. I think that with another jack, other than in diamonds, I would choose to bid three spades.

Of less consequence, I do not care for the three diamond bid by East. He found his partner with a useful minimum and they still went down. With suitable defense and only three diamonds, East should let it go.

49

♠ 10 2
♡ 8 7 3
◇ A 7 4
♣ J 10 7 6 3

We are not vul versus vul. LHO passes and partner opens
ONE CLUB. RHO DOUBLES. I raise to TWO CLUBS only
because I want to tell partner I have something. I certainly am
not bidding three clubs on this balanced minimum. LHO bids
TWO HEARTS, partner passes, and RHO bids TWO
NOTRUMP. These are sound opponents, so I expect East to
have a good hand. LHO rebids THREE HEARTS and RHO
continues to FOUR HEARTS.

Dealer: West
Vul: East-West

WEST	NORTH	EAST	SOUTH
Pass	1 ♣	Double	2 ♣
2 ♡	Pass	2 NT	Pass
3 ♡	Pass	4 ♡	Pass
Pass	Pass		

Partner leads the club king.

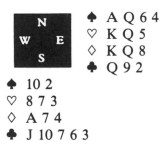

♠ A Q 6 4
♡ K Q 5
◇ K Q 8
♣ Q 9 2

♠ 10 2
♡ 8 7 3
◇ A 7 4
♣ J 10 7 6 3

The club king wins as the rest of us play two, three and the
four. Partner switches to the jack of spades, won by dummy's
queen. Declarer plays the heart king, queen and five to his ace.

Partner follows twice with the four and jack and discards the club five. Declarer leads the three of diamonds to partner's two, dummy's king and my four. It's possible declarer has the ten-nine of diamonds. Then ducking will leave him with a guess. I don't think if declarer has a guess that it will be a difficult one, but it can't hurt to try. When dummy continues with the queen, I win, declarer and partner playing the five and six.

What now?

What is happening?

So far, partner has shown up with two hearts, which guarantees he has four clubs. There is no distribution with two hearts which would be opened one club with a three card suit. Partner's two-six of diamonds implies three but does not guarantee it. He could have four. He cannot have two diamonds because that would leave him with 5-2-2-4 and this would not be opened one club. Partner's high cards so far have included the heart jack and the club ace-king. I can't believe he has the jack of diamonds. That would mean declarer has played diamonds in a most unusual fashion. Therefore, partner has the king of spades for his opening bid and the jack of spades which he led at trick two.

What should I return now?

It is pretty easy to lead a club back. Right? Wrong?

If declarer has

♠ xxxx   he will pitch one spade on the club return. Then
♡ Axxxx   he will pitch another spade on the club queen
◇ Jxx   and claim.
♣ x

If declarer has

♠ xxx   he will ruff the club and will run off his winners.
♡ Axxxx   This will squeeze partner out of his club ace or
◇ J10xx   his spade guard. That will permit an overtrick.
♣ x

This means that regardless of which hand declarer has, a club return cannot gain and may lose. A spade return however can only break even or better. In the first setup, it doesn't matter, but in the second one, it will remove the spade communication and the squeeze will fail.

This turns out to be the actual hand. The spade return was necessary.

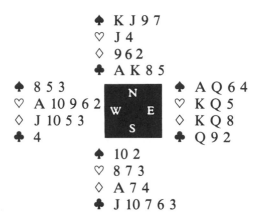

```
              ♠ K J 9 7
              ♡ J 4
              ◇ 9 6 2
              ♣ A K 8 5
  ♠ 8 5 3                    ♠ A Q 6 4
  ♡ A 10 9 6 2   N           ♡ K Q 5
  ◇ J 10 5 3   W   E         ◇ K Q 8
  ♣ 4           S            ♣ Q 9 2
              ♠ 10 2
              ♡ 8 7 3
              ◇ A 7 4
              ♣ J 10 7 6 3
```

Some good things happened here. Partner had to shift to a spade at trick one and then South had to return one later to break up the squeeze.

FURTHER ANALYSIS

As a defender, when you find yourself in a position where you seem to have one more trick coming, you should give a little thought to this hand. Is your trick immediately available? Then go ahead and take it. But if you judge that the trick is a slow one, then don't be guilty of lazy defense. If you look for ways the trick may escape, you may be able to avoid a disaster.

50

♠ 2
♡ Q 8 6 4 2
◇ 8 7
♣ A K 10 6 3

Our side is vulnerable and my RHO opens with TWO CLUBS, their strong bid. If the vulnerability were reversed I would certainly get into the auction. As it is, I can still make a token contribution. I DOUBLE, showing good clubs. LHO passes as does partner. Opener bids TWO SPADES and LHO THREE HEARTS. When opener bids FOUR DIAMONDS. I have momentary hopes that they have a total misfit. No, LHO prefers to FOUR SPADES. This is enough for opener to bid a Blackwood FOUR NOTRUMP. Over the FIVE DIAMOND response, opener leaps to SIX SPADES which becomes the final contract.

Dealer: East
Vul: North-South

EAST	SOUTH	WEST	NORTH
2 ♣	Double	Pass	Pass
2 ♠	Pass	3 ♡	Pass
4 ◇	Pass	4 ♠	Pass
4 NT	Pass	5 ◇	Pass
6 ♠	Pass	Pass	Pass

♠ 9 5
♡ A J 9 7
◇ 10 9 4
♣ 9 8 5 2

```
      N
   W     E
      S
```

♠ 2
♡ Q 8 6 4 2
◇ 8 7
♣ A K 10 6 3

I lead the king of clubs which wins, the play going two, seven, and jack. I don't think there is any question that declarer has exactly one club, and I consider if leading another club might help declarer by shortening his trumps. Our most likely second trick is in trumps, if partner has queen third or jack fourth. Declarer will have to guess the first holding, and may need some sort of trump coup for the second. But since my partner might have five small spades, I decide to continue clubs. If partner does have five small, we will need to tap declarer.

At trick two, I lead the ace of clubs which declarer ruffs. He follows with the ace and king of spades and, when I show out, he goes into the closet for some serious thinking.

What is he thinking about?

Either he is clearly going down, and he is trying to minimize his losses, or he is thinking of some way to make six spades.

Can I tell which it is?

Yes. This declarer is showing definite signs of interest in his hand. There is none of the despair or lack of interest or intensity that one would expect if the contract were now impossible.

What is happening?

It depends on the quality of your opponent, and this one I know to be quite competent. Assuming that declarer is trying to make this hand, he must have exactly six spades. If he had five, he would be going down, and if he had seven, then my partner would either have a sure spade trick, with queen third, or no chance of a spade trick. Declarer must have six spades AKQ10xx and is considering some way to pick up partner's remaining Jx.

What is declarer's shape?

Probably 6-2-4-1. For a trump coup to succeed declarer will have to cash all his side winners without drawing any more trumps. If he has five diamonds he will need to find North, my partner, with five diamonds as well. This unlikely split of course does not exist.

I expect declarer to have approximately:

♠ AKQ10xx
♡ Kx
◇ AKQx
♣ x

His diamonds could be AKJx or AKQJ. I don't expect any other variation.

Declarer cashes the ace of diamonds and, when everyone follows, shows no signs of disappointment. I interpret this as confirmation that is 6-4.

How is declarer going to make this if I have correctly judged his hand?

He will enter dummy twice. First he will ruff a club. Then, after taking his winners, he will enter dummy a second time at trick eleven and partner will be couped.

What are declarer's two entries? The only possible entries are the jack and ace of hearts. If the ten of diamonds is an entry, it will mean declarer has five diamonds, and there cannot be a coup.

Is there anything I can do about this?

While I am contemplating, declarer leads the five of hearts. Is there anything I can do? Is this the time?

If declarer has the hand I think he has, then I can deny him the second entry to dummy.

What does this mean?

If I had gauged declarer's hand correctly it will include the doubleton king of hearts. King-five, to be exact. His intention is to finesse the jack of hearts for his first entry, and later to over-take the king of hearts for his second entry. I can upset this plan by inserting the queen. Declarer will win the ace, but will not have another dummy entry.

I put in the queen and declarer ultimately concedes down one.

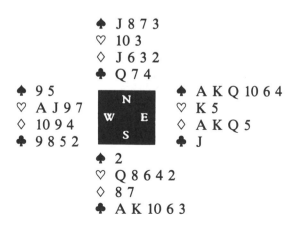

FURTHER ANALYSIS

This entry-denying play is rather rare, but those occasions where it is necessary are reasonably obvious. The situation will be one where declarer is strapped for entries.

This does not occur only at trump contracts; it could just as easily occur at notrump. In the above hand, declarer needed entries to manage a trump coup. But declarer might also need entries to take a finesse, to set up a suit, or make any of an endless variety of plays.

Here are a few examples of suit positions which offer an opportunity for this sort of play.

A. AJ42   This is the example just discussed. LHO inserted
    K5   the queen when the five was led.

B. A104   In this setup, LHO had led the suit and RHO
    Q76   won the king. If declarer needs entries to dummy, he will throw the queen on the king. Then he
C. A10   will be able to finesse the ten. Failure to unblock
    Q7   the queen will leave position C. If declarer now attempts to lead the seven to the ten, LHO can play the jack, restricting South to one entry.

D. AQ10   In position D, declarer must also use a little care.
    K43   If South needs three entries to dummy, he better start with the king to dummy's ace. Carelessly
E. A10   leading the three to the queen, will leave position
    K4   E. LHO, once again, can frustrate declarer by playing the jack when he tries to lead the four to the ten.

There are some interesting aspects to the play of this hand. Here is the problem from declarer's point of view.

♠ 9 5
♡ A J 9 7
◇ 10 9 4
♣ 9 8 5 2

♠ A K Q 10 6 4
♡ K 5
◇ A K Q 5
♣ J

Declarer ruffed the second round of clubs and then discovered RHO had Jxxx of spades. To make this hand he had to get to dummy, ruff a club, cash four diamonds, and then get back to dummy by overtaking the heart king.

Notice that this plan requires the cashing of four diamonds. It will not suffice to find the diamonds three-three because the fourth round, though good, would be ruffed. In order to cash four diamonds declarer would have to find one of two setups. He could play LHO for Jx, and play ace, king, over to the ten, and later cash the queen. Or he could play RHO for Jxxx, in which case he will have to take a diamond finesse! Declarer has to guess which lie to play for.

Our declarer was playing RHO for Jxxx which is twice as likely as finding LHO with Jx.

Note that declarer's line of play was mildly insulting. By choosing to play as he did, he was subject to defeat whenever the heart queen was offside or whenever LHO played it the first time hearts were led. From this point of view, he could never make six spades. The alternative of playing for Jx in LHO's hand could not be defeated if LHO did have Jx. Declarer was playing for a defensive error plus a certain division of diamonds. It is difficult to determine which is the better line at the table.

One other combination of diamonds was mentioned, AKJx. With this holding, declarer could not make six spades if RHO had Qxxx because he could not both ruff a club and take the two diamond finesses necessitated by RHO's diamond length.

Therefore, his correct play would be to play the ace-king of diamonds hoping for Qx on his left. Now he would have the needed second dummy entry in the ten of diamonds.

The full analysis of this hand is even more involved than I have so far implied. It would use two or three times the space already taken.

On the actual hand, declarer could not have made six spades in any circumstance had the defense not played a second club. Perhaps my partner with Q74 of clubs should play the four instead of the seven. If I switch at trick two, declarer will surely fail unless he takes a spade finesse.

But then if clubs are not continued, any switch will look very suspicious. Why did the defense not continue clubs? Perhaps declarer would work out the reason. Or would he suspect a double cross?

51

♠ A 6 3
♡ K 8 4
◇ A 10 3
♣ 9 7 4 2

No one is vulnerable and, once again, neither partner nor I are able to get into the auction. Partner deals and passes and RHO opens ONE DIAMOND. The auction continues:

Dealer: North
Vul: None

NORTH	EAST	SOUTH	WEST
Pass	1 ◇	Pass	1 ♠
Pass	2 ♠	Pass	4 ♠
Pass	Pass	Pass	

Partner leads the five of clubs, and I think I don't like this lead.

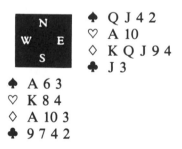

♠ Q J 4 2
♡ A 10
◇ K Q J 9 4
♣ J 3

♠ A 6 3
♡ K 8 4
◇ A 10 3
♣ 9 7 4 2

When dummy wins with the jack, I am sure I don't like it. Either partner has led from the king, costing us a club trick or he has led from the queen which will ultimately cost us a heart trick, as declarer can now pitch dummy's ten of hearts. Declarer follows with dummy's queen of spades, which I duck, and continues with the two of spades. This one I take, trusting partner hasn't ducked with Kx. Partner who followed once, discards the three of hearts.

How should I continue?

I can exit safely with a club or a spade or I can attack with a heart. I can't see any reason to lead a diamond.

Which is right?

The answer to this, as so often is the case, is determined by ascertaining how many tricks declarer has.

How many does he have?

He has four spades, one heart, four diamonds (unless he is void) and two clubs plus a club ruff in dummy. This actually adds up to twelve tricks.

Well, he is not going to get twelve, but he certainly has the means to get eleven.

What does this dictate?

Since declarer has eleven tricks if left to his own devices, it is necessary to establish a trick. This can only come from the heart suit. So I switch to the four of hearts. If partner has the queen, we will set up a trick. If he has the jack, we will set up a trick if declarer misguesses.

Of course if declarer has the ace and king of clubs, this is just an exercise.

Can the heart shift cost a trick?

Very unlikely. Only if declarer is void in diamonds can this switch cost.

Declarer takes his time deciding what to play, so I expect he has the queen. Since he has a problem, he probably does not have the ace and king of clubs.

I'm not sure that he has sufficient inferences to do the right thing here. I am rooting for him to play low. Perhaps that will help.

Maybe it did. Declarer plays low and partner's jack forces the ace. When I get in with the diamond ace, the heart king holds them to ten tricks.

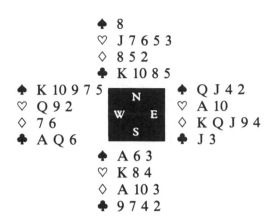

```
                  ♠ 8
                  ♡ J 7 6 5 3
                  ◊ 8 5 2
                  ♣ K 10 8 5
  ♠ K 10 9 7 5                      ♠ Q J 4 2
  ♡ Q 9 2          N               ♡ A 10
  ◊ 7 6        W       E           ◊ K Q J 9 4
  ♣ A Q 6          S               ♣ J 3
                  ♠ A 6 3
                  ♡ K 8 4
                  ◊ A 10 3
                  ♣ 9 7 4 2
```

Even though we could not beat four spades after the opening lead, the principle used to hold them to four is still valid. There will be many cases where the setting trick is at stake.

I have nothing but sympathy for partner's opening lead. Against strong auctions it is usually best to attack. I would consider no other lead from partner's hand.

52

♠ K Q 4
♡ 10 8 5
◇ J 9 6 4
♣ A Q 7

Everyone is vulnerable, and RHO opens ONE DIAMOND. I pass and LHO responds ONE HEART. Opener bids TWO CLUBS. My hand is looking good defensively and even though we aren't going to play the hand, I am beginning to entertain thoughts of a plus score.

When LHO continues with TWO NOTRUMP, opener raises confidently to THREE NOTRUMP. I have some hopes of beating this, but under no circumstances would I double. I want partner to make his normal lead, and if it happens to be a spade, I don't want him to change his mind.

Dealer: East
Vul: Both

EAST	SOUTH	WEST	NORTH
1 ◇	Pass	1 ♡	Pass
2 ♣	Pass	2 NT	Pass
3 NT	Pass	Pass	Pass

Partner does have a preference for spades it turns out, leading the two.

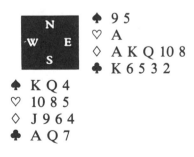

♠ 9 5
♡ A
◇ A K Q 10 8
♣ K 6 5 3 2

♠ K Q 4
♡ 10 8 5
◇ J 9 6 4
♣ A Q 7

Declarer gives the hand a bit more than the usual trick one pause and plays the five from dummy. My queen wins, and when I continue with the king, that wins too.

Are we going to kill this?

If partner wins the next spade and returns a club, we will get three or four spades, two clubs and maybe a diamond. Right?

I'm not so sure. Does partner have the ace of spades? Or is declarer holding up? If so, it seems a little peculiar.

I am inclined to give declarer the ace of spades. Why? Because I'm looking at twenty eight high card points which leaves only twelve unaccounted for. Declarer, without the ace of spades would have a poor eight. I think he has the ace and my partner the jack. Perhaps my partner has another jack, but I can't expect him to have any more.

Why is declarer playing as he is? Does it matter? Should I just exit with a spade, or should I do something else?

I think a switch to hearts is clear. There are more reasons for this than immediately meet the eye. First, by switching to hearts, I may be able to create a dummy lock! If I can keep declarer from getting to his hand, I will get two clubs and a diamond, plus the two spades already in. The second reason is that I suspect declarer has the remaining high cards which include the KQ of hearts at least and maybe the KQJ9(x). If I lead another spade, declarer will win and will discard dummy's ace of hearts! If his hearts are, in fact, KQJ9(x) he will score them up.

I am not going to give declarer this option. No more spades. I'm exiting with a heart, and need only decide which one.

Well?

It is unlikely to matter since partner won't be getting in, but on the off chance he does, I lead the ten of hearts to tell him I have no interest in the suit.

Dummy wins the heart lead with the ace, my partner playing the two. I can infer from this that he has bad hearts, but for the moment, I don't know how many he has. When declarer next calls for the two of clubs I have an agonizing decision.

I can play the queen and ace of clubs and then try to put dummy in with the club seven. This will work whenever declarer has two or fewer clubs. Or I can duck, playing partner for the jack. Even if partner doesn't have the jack, a duck could be right if declarer has J9x. If I play low, declarer might finesse the nine. This would be a very reasonable play.

Can I tell?

Maybe I can, maybe not.

I don't see how I can tell on the basis of what I've seen.

I wish I had given more thought to this in advance. If, before I led a heart, I had anticipated this problem, I would be much better placed.

I finally decide to duck on a rather weak premise. It's right if declarer is 4-4-2-3 or 4-5-1-3 which seem more likely than 4-5-2-2 or 4-4-3-2. With one of these last two hands declarer might cash the diamond suit before leading clubs.

Declarer puts the nine on my seven and partner beats this with the ten.

I'm glad I led the ten of hearts. It's surprising how these things come home to roost. Partner seems to have worked out what's happening because he returns the five of diamonds. Now, regardless of declarer's play, I will get two clubs or one club and one diamond.

One down.

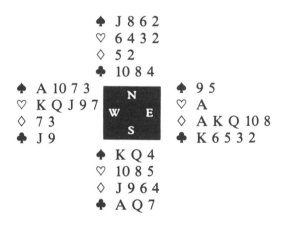

```
                    ♠ J 8 6 2
                    ♡ 6 4 3 2
                    ◇ 5 2
                    ♣ 10 8 4
    ♠ A 10 7 3              ♠ 9 5
    ♡ K Q J 9 7            ♡ A
    ◇ 7 3                  ◇ A K Q 10 8
    ♣ J 9                 ♣ K 6 5 3 2
                    ♠ K Q 4
                    ♡ 10 8 5
                    ◇ J 9 6 4
                    ♣ A Q 7
```

While I am hardly sure of the proper play in clubs, there were other important and well-defined points of interest on this hand.

I note that declarer did have 4-5-2-2 and my play could have cost the contract. Perhaps I was lucky.

FURTHER ANALYSIS

Two points are worth emphasizing. First is the importance of

177

returning the ten of hearts to imply no interest in the suit.

And second is the wisdom of thinking abour forseeable problems in advance. I would prefer, for instance, to have played a low club more easily than I did. It turns out not to have cost, but...

53

♠ K 10 7 3 2
♡ 10 6 5
◇ A J 5
♣ 10 8

No one is vul and RHO opens TWO NOTRUMP. I pass and LHO raises to THREE NOTRUMP, making it my lead.

Dealer: East
Vul: None

EAST	SOUTH	WEST	NORTH
2 NT	Pass	3 NT	Pass
Pass	Pass		

I can think of no reason not to lead the three of spades, so I do so, with some optimism.

♠ Q 5
♡ Q J 4
◇ Q 9 7 6 3
♣ J 5 4

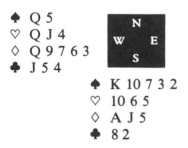

♠ K 10 7 3 2
♡ 10 6 5
◇ A J 5
♣ 8 2

Dummy goes up with the queen which wins, my partner offering the nine. As expected, declarer plays diamonds, leading the three to partner's two and his king.

What's going to happen? Can we beat three notrump?

Unlikely. Declarer's bid shows twenty one or twenty two points, so my partner doesn't have much. At best, he can have three points.

What should I make of partner's nine of spades? There are various interpretations. One is count, in which case I would credit partner with two or four spades. Another possibility is the Foster echo. Using this my partner will play his second highest card whenever he can't beat dummy's card. If we were using this convention, I could trust partner to have the jack of spades, but I would have no idea of his spade length. Third, partner's nine could be used as a signal to say that he had a useful card in the suit led. This time the useful card could only be the jack.

My understanding with this partner is that we are using the third system of signals. With other partners, I am willing to use the first system, giving count. With no one will I play the Foster echo. All too often partner's discard cannot be interpreted. For instance, if he played the six, I would not know whether he had

J6	or
J64	or
96	or
964	or
86	or
864.	

Hopeless.

Anyway. Partner's nine of spades guarantees the jack, so I now know partner has at most another queen and may not have that. Therefore, I can count declarer for two spades, from three to five hearts, a diamond, and two or more club tricks. It is possible declarer hasn't nine tricks, but that is unlikely.

Should I win the diamond ace?

If I do, I will continue spades and declarer will win the next round if he has two, or he may choose to duck a round if he has three. Then he can duck a diamond into my partner who will have no more spades and end up with ten tricks. This assumes that my partner has the ten of diamonds.

Curiously, it is possible that ducking the diamond is right.

How does this work? Can't declarer just lead a diamond to the queen?

If I have ducked smoothly enough, declarer may judge the ace to be in my partner's hand. When he leads another diamond toward the queen, I will play the jack. One of two things will happen. If declarer has the ten of diamonds, he will cover my jack and will likely take the rest of the tricks except for the diamond ace. But then, he might take them anyway. However, if declarer does not have the ten of diamonds, he may duck in dummy hoping my partner has the doubleton ace.

This will permit me to win and clear the spade suit. Then, if declarer decides to lead more diamonds he will be surprised to find that I have the ace along with the rest of the spades.

I put this plan into effect, playing the five on the king.

When declarer leads the eight towards the dummy, I play the jack. This is the crucial moment. I will be quite embarrassed if declarer started with K108x of diamonds.

This is not the case obviously, as declarer is not calling for the queen with the air of a man whose problems are over. But he isn't ducking either. Does he suspect? Well, he may be suspicious, but he isn't that suspicious. He ducks and my partner plays the ten.

I'm going back to spades and I lead the two. If I had the K10832 of spades I would lead the king to allow for J9 only in partner's hand. But with K10732 I cannot afford this. I could, if I wanted, lead the seven, but there is a good reason not to.

Which is?

Since declarer apparently thinks my partner has the ace of diamonds, I want him to know that I have five spades. If he has three spades, he may judge to hold up. Then, by his lights, he can give my partner the ace of diamonds and claim the balance.

Why does it matter that he thinks the spades are five-three and the ace of diamonds is with my partner? Won't he lead another diamond anyway?

Not if he has nine tricks. If he has only eight, he will probably choose to lead a diamond, his alternative being a club finesse, playing my partner for the queen.

Or perhaps declarer does have nine tricks. If he is a greedy declarer, he might lead a diamond trying for an overtrick.

Declarer in the meantime ducks my spade return and when partner produces a third spade, declarer takes it.

At this stage whatever happens will happen. We have done all we can. What will declarer do?

Good news. Declarer leads a diamond. This results in a rapid down one.

Better news. Declarer had nine tricks on top. Greedy. Even better news. Dummy is explaining why declarer should go up with the queen of diamonds earlier and why he should never had led that last round. I wonder how well this partnership will perform on ensuing hands.

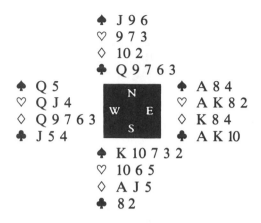

♠ J 9 6
♥ 9 7 3
♦ 10 2
♣ Q 9 7 6 3

♠ Q 5   N   ♠ A 8 4
♥ Q J 4   W   E   ♥ A K 8 2
♦ Q 9 7 6 3   S   ♦ K 8 4
♣ J 5 4   ♣ A K 10

♠ K 10 7 3 2
♥ 10 6 5
♦ A J 5
♣ 8 2

FURTHER ANALYSIS

I note that this coup would have no chance if my partner automatically gave count. This may seem trivial but I have seen defenders righteously play the ten of diamonds in similar situations.

I have not stated the form of bridge being played. At IMPs or rubber bridge, a good declarer would take his nine tricks rather than undertake the dangerous and greedy effort for an overtrick. At matchpoints, the play for an overtrick would have more merit.

Nonetheless the concept is sound. Say the cards were rearranged slightly.

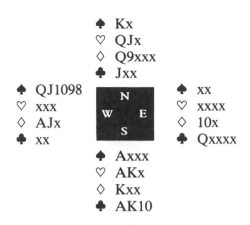

♠ Kx
♡ QJx
◇ Q9xxx
♣ Jxx

♠ QJ1098
♡ xxx
◇ AJx
♣ xx

♠ xx
♡ xxxx
◇ 10x
♣ Qxxxx

♠ Axxx
♡ AKx
◇ Kxx
♣ AK10

In this setup declarer wins the spade king, wins the diamond king, and loses a diamond to LHO's jack. At this stage declarer has eight tricks and can take a club finesse for nine or can concede a diamond for ten. I think most declarers would opt for the diamond play.

This play, if attempted, must be anticipated and made with no hesitation. Also, you must have no reason to think that declarer has length in the suit being played. On the hand discussed, it was reasonable to hope partner had two or more diamonds. But if the auction had suggested declarer had four diamonds, the play would be silly.

54

♠ 9 4
♡ A 10 5
◇ 10 8 6 4
♣ 10 9 7 2

With no one vulnerable, my RHO opens TWO CLUBS. My LHO gives the negative reply of TWO DIAMONDS, which is alerted. While tentatively weak, it seems that LHO may have a good hand. We'll see. RHO rebids TWO NOTRUMP showing 23 or 24 but maybe a great 22. LHO bids THREE CLUBS, asking for a major suit. Opener has one, and bids THREE SPADES. This is raised to FOUR SPADES and it becomes my lead.

Dealer: East
Vul: None

EAST	SOUTH	WEST	NORTH
2 ♣	Pass	2 ◇	Pass
2 NT	Pass	3 ♣	Pass
3 ♠	Pass	4 ♠	Pass
Pass	Pass		

I ask and find out opener does not have four hearts also.

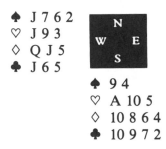

♠ J 7 6 2
♡ J 9 3
◇ Q J 5
♣ J 6 5

♠ 9 4
♡ A 10 5
◇ 10 8 6 4
♣ 10 9 7 2

I lead the ten of clubs which goes to partner's ace. He returns the eight to declarer's king. Next come the ace and king of spades, partner playing the eight and the ten. Declarer now plays the ace and king of diamonds and a diamond to dummy's queen, partner following. A club is led to declarer's hand, and again no one shows out. Declarer leads a spade to partner's queen, and partner, with nothing left but hearts, leads the two. Declarer plays the four and it is my turn.

I seem to have two options. I can win and return a heart, or I can duck. I am not going to win and give a sluff and a ruff.

Which option should I select?

And why?

Perhaps reconstructing the hand will help.

What is declarer's shape?

He is guaranteed to be 4-3-3-3. I have seen all the clubs and diamonds and I know declarer has exactly four spades.

What about the high cards?

The auction says that partner can have up to seven points, although if declarer has only twenty-two, then my partner has eight.

Can partner have the king of hearts?

No. He has shown up with the spade queen and the club ace. If he had the heart king, it would leave declarer with twenty-one points.

Can he have the heart queen?

This is just barely possible in theory, but quite likely in practice. If declarer had the queen of hearts, he wouldn't be wasting time. I'm going to defend on the assumption that partner has the queen. Perhaps my play won't make any difference, but I'm going to consider all my options.

What happens if I take the ace?

I will have to lead a heart back. Declarer will play the nine and we will not get a second heart trick.

What happens if I play the ten?

Dummy will win the jack and lead a heart. If my partner has the Q8, he will play the eight, declarer the king, and we will have two heart tricks. Good enough.

Unless partner doesn't have the eight. If declarer has it, he will finesse it on the second round of hearts, holding us to one heart trick.

Still, the ten of hearts can get a second trick some of the time so it is a better play than the ace.

And what happens if I duck the heart altogether?

This looks like the winner. Declarer will win the nine. Now, regardless of how he continues, he will lose two heart tricks as long as we don't do anything foolish.

Since declarer is still making no motions to claim, I think that perhaps these moments of reflection have been well spent. I play the five and have not long to wait to see if it matters.

It did.

The complete hand is as I hoped:

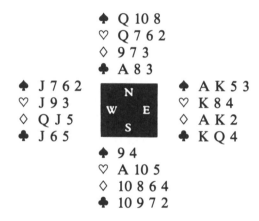

55

♠ 8 4
♡ Q J
◇ A 9 8 6 4
♣ 8 7 3 2

We are not vulnerable against vul, and LHO starts with ONE CLUB. RHO responds ONE HEART and opener rebids ONE SPADE. This seems to be their suit for responder leaps to THREE SPADES and opener continues to FOUR SPADES.

Dealer: West
Vul: East-West

WEST	NORTH	EAST	SOUTH
1 ♣	Pass	1 ♡	Pass
1 ♠	Pass	3 ♠	Pass
4 ♠	Pass	Pass	Pass

My partner starts with the queen of diamonds which looks like it might be good for us. Dummy, however, has two small diamonds, so the lead is not the success I had hoped for. Conversely, though, dummy's hearts are such that my own hearts suddenly acquire more value.

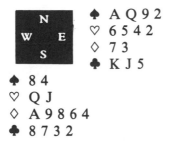

♠ A Q 9 2
♡ 6 5 4 2
◇ 7 3
♣ K J 5

♠ 8 4
♡ Q J
◇ A 9 8 6 4
♣ 8 7 3 2

I win the ace of diamonds and declarer follows with the two. Before deciding on my next play, I ask if three spades was forcing or limit. Usually when you see a hand you can tell, but this time it's not so clear. Declarer says it's limit, so I can assume he has a bit more than a minimum.

At trick two I switch to the queen of hearts. Perhaps we will have better luck in hearts than in diamonds.

No. Declarer takes the ace as partner encourages with the nine.

Declarer leads the spade jack, covered by partner's king. Two more rounds of trump are drawn, partner showing up with K65. On the third round of trumps I have to make a discard.

Can I do something constructive, or is this a hand where I should mind my own business and let everyone else go about theirs?

Perhaps nothing matters, but it can't hurt to check.

What do I know so far?

I know partner has exactly Kxx of spades.

I know partner has at least four hearts to the king.

What heart spots does he have?

He has K98x(x). If he had the 10, he would have played it on the theory that you make your discards as emphatic as possible.

Why can't partner have three hearts?

Because opener would have four and would have raised.

Can partner have five hearts?

It's possible, but if so, that would leave him with

♠ Kxx
♡ K98xx
♦ QJx(x)
♣ x(x)

and he might have overcalled.

I'm pretty sure partner has exactly four hearts.

How about clubs? Can partner have a club honor?

Not likely. Declarer bid four spades on an invitational sequence. So far he has shown up with

♠ J10xx	Known
♡ A10x	Implied
◇ Kx	Probable
♣ AQxx	Without both honors he would pass three spades.

If my construction is correct, what is there for me to do?

There is a serious danger here. If declarer has the above hand he will take his winners and will lead a heart. I will win my jack, but will have to give a sluff and ruff, permitting declarer to discard his heart loser.

What can I do about this?

What I can do is discard the jack of hearts. Now if the play goes as I think it will, my partner will be able to take two heart tricks. This will not set them, but it will hold declarer to the minimum number of tricks.

I try the effect of this play and it works out exactly as hoped. This is the complete hand:

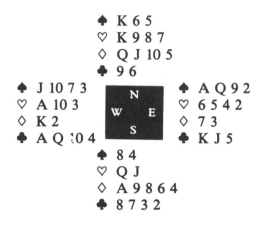

♠ K 6 5
♥ K 9 8 7
♦ Q J 10 5
♣ 9 6

♠ J 10 7 3
♥ A 10 3
♦ K 2
♣ A Q 10 4

♠ A Q 9 2
♥ 6 5 4 2
♦ 7 3
♣ K J 5

♠ 8 4
♥ Q J
♦ A 9 8 6 4
♣ 8 7 3 2

FURTHER ANALYSIS

This position is not all that uncommon. It occurs whenever the defense has two tricks to cash which cannot be taken immediately because one of the winners is singleton.

Sometimes the condition exists when the hand begins. And sometimes it evolves as it did in the example hand.

Here is another typical case.

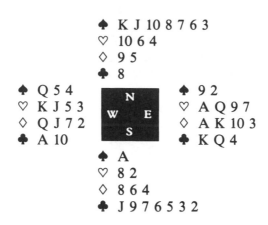

```
                ♠ K J 10 8 7 6 3
                ♡ 10 6 4
                ◇ 9 5
                ♣ 8
  ♠ Q 5 4          N          ♠ 9 2
  ♡ K J 5 3                   ♡ A Q 9 7
  ◇ Q J 7 2    W       E      ◇ A K 10 3
  ♣ A 10          S          ♣ K Q 4
                ♠ A
                ♡ 8 2
                ◇ 8 6 4
                ♣ J 9 7 6 5 3 2
```

West opened one heart and North preempted three spades. This had the effect of driving East to six hearts. North chose to lead the eight of clubs and when declarer drew trumps it was necessary for South to dump the ace of spades. Failure to do so would result in South's being stuck in with it and being forced to give a ruff-discard.

Note that in my analysis I cited

```
                ♠ Kxx
                ♡ K98xx
                ◇ QJx
                ♣ xx
```

as one of my partner's possible hands and then rejected it because partner might have overcalled.

I am not necessarily saying that this is an overcall. However, if you know that your partner of the moment thinks it is, then you can use the knowledge in evaluating what partner does or does not have.

56

♠ 3 2
♡ 6 4 2
◇ K J 9 5 2
♣ K 9 4

We are vulnerable, so when RHO opens ONE CLUB, I am not tempted to do anything rash. LHO responds ONE HEART and opener rebids ONE NOTRUMP. LHO gives a jump raise to THREE CLUBS but opener returns to THREE NOTRUMP. It is passed out and I am on lead.

This does not look like a time to try the "unbid major" so I start with the five of diamonds. We might well be able to take the first five tricks.

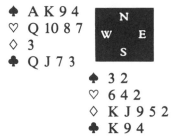

♠ A K 9 4
♡ Q 10 8 7
◇ 3
♣ Q J 7 3

♠ 3 2
♡ 6 4 2
◇ K J 9 5 2
♣ K 9 4

Dealer: East
Vul: North-South

EAST	SOUTH	WEST	NORTH
1 ♣	Pass	1 ♡	Pass
1 NT	Pass	3 ♣	Pass
3 NT	Pass	Pass	Pass

At trick one, partner plays the queen, taken by the ace. This leaves us in good position.

Declarer leads the ten of spades to dummy's king and partner's five, and then the queen of clubs to partner's six and his two.

Should I take this?

It probably does not matter. Ducking would lose if declarer

could take nine tricks now, but I doubt that he can.

What does ducking gain?

Usually you duck when you want to cut off entries to the suit, or when you wish declarer to use entries to repeat an apparently winning finesse.

Here all you have to gain is the knowledge that partner does or does not have another club and whatever he may convey with his discard when he does have just one club.

In practice, I am tempted by my four potential diamond tricks so I take the first club and start the diamonds.

Which diamond should I lead? Does it matter?

Yes. There are at least four diamond positions I must cater to.

I must read this position accurately and lead diamonds from the top.	3 KJ952 Q864 A107	

I must cash only one diamond and then, if possible, get partner in to return his last diamond.	3 KJ952 Q84 A1076	

I must guess to lead diamonds from the top, as in the first example.	3 KJ952 Q104 A876	

I must not permit partner's ten of diamonds to block the suit, I must determine if he has it, and must convince him to play it early, or I must guess to underlead to it while he still has one to return.	3 KJ952 Q1064 A87	

How can I cater to these various possible holdings?

I am surely not about to underlead my KJ of diamonds, so I

need only to consider the effect of leading the king as opposed to the jack. Obviously either will win, but I wonder if partner will treat both the same way.

For instance, if partner started with Q1064, what will he do if I lead the king?

I think what he will do is play the four. Then on the jack, he will have to decide whether or not to unblock the ten.

3

KJ852   .   Q1064

A97

In this setup, partner would have to unblock the ten if I lead the king and jack.

3

KJ85   Q1064

A972

In this setup, partner should not unblock the ten.

It seems to me that the king can lead to some confusion.

By comparison, I think the jack should clear things up. When partner has the ten, it should alert him that something unusual is up. He should conclude that I want him to play the ten if he has it. If he does not have it he will give count. I cannot think of a combination where this will fail unless partner misinterprets my intentions.

I do lead the jack and partner plays the eight. This shows no ten and, I assume, he is showing an even number of diamonds at this point.

He probably has Q8x, but could he possibly have Q8xxx? It would be silly not to run diamonds when holding ten of them.

No. This can't be.

First, declarer would have A10 doubleton, and declarer has just played the six. Second, declarer with a doubleton diamond would have bid a major suit somewhere along the line.

193

Since I know diamonds aren't running, I have to shift to a major or exit safely with a club.

What do I know about spades? Should I lead one?

I think declarer has Q10x of spades. With J10x he might not have bid notrump so many times and he might have led the jack rather than the ten. If he has Q108, a spade lead will give up a trick. That would leave partner with J765 and I wouldn't expect him to give automatic count in this situation.

Should I exit with a heart? I think so. If partner has the ace, we clean up fast. If not, I will be doing nothing for declarer that he couldn't do for himself.

A club is dangerous in that declarer might now have nine tricks, if he has, say:

♠ QJ10
♡ K
◇ A10xx
♣ Axxxx

I don't expect this but there is no reason to give declarer a free ride.

After consideration, I shift to the six of hearts. I lead the six to imply no heart honor. I don't want partner to think I have a high card in the suit.

The play goes to dummy's ten, partner's jack, and declarer's ace. Declarer takes some black winners, but soon my partner gets in and we can cash out for down one.

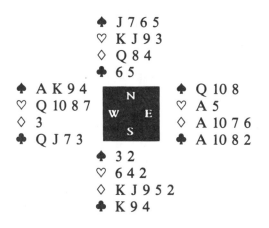

```
                    ♠ J 7 6 5
                    ♡ K J 9 3
                    ◇ Q 8 4
                    ♣ 6 5
    ♠ A K 9 4                        ♠ Q 10 8
    ♡ Q 10 8 7       N               ♡ A 5
    ◇ 3          W        E          ◇ A 10 7 6
    ♣ Q J 7 3        S               ♣ A 10 8 2
                    ♠ 3 2
                    ♡ 6 4 2
                    ◇ K J 9 5 2
                    ♣ K 9 4
```

194

The play of the diamond jack has some similarities to the lead of the queen from KQ10(9)(x). Some players use the queen to ask partner either to drop the jack or to give count.

FURTHER ANALYSIS

I mentioned that partner would not give count in spades. There are many reasons why and when he should and shouldn't. In this case declarer rebid one notrump and his spade length is reasonably well-known to the defense.

However if you are playing against someone who is likely to suppress a four card major in this auction, then the defense might try harder to give count to clear up possible ambiguities.

Do people still bid this way?

Yes. Eddie Kantar does when he plays with anyone. And I do it when I play with Eddie.

As an exercise you should compare how you would defend holding various diamond combinations when partner leads the king as opposed to the jack as in the example hand.

57

♠ Q 10 8 7 2
♡ Q J 10
♢ A 9
♣ 9 5 3

Both sides are vulnerable and my LHO opens ONE CLUB. RHO responds ONE DIAMOND. Bidding has little to gain so I pass. LHO rebids TWO CLUBS and RHO jumps to THREE DIAMONDS. Opener converts to THREE NOTRUMP and when it is passed out, partner asks if three diamonds was forcing. It was not.

Dealer: West
Vul: Both

WEST	NORTH	EAST	SOUTH
1 ♣	Pass	1 ♢	Pass
2 ♣	Pass	3 ♢	Pass
3 NT	Pass	Pass	Pass

Partner leads the five of hearts.

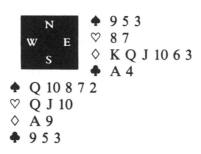

♠ 9 5 3
♡ 8 7
♢ K Q J 10 6 3
♣ A 4

♠ Q 10 8 7 2
♡ Q J 10
♢ A 9
♣ 9 5 3

I play the jack and declarer wins the king. His diamond two goes to partner's five and dummy's king.
Should I take this?
Absolutely!
Who so emphatic?
Because they are going down if we cash out.

What tricks do we have for sure? Hearts? Spades?

Hearts. Partner's five of hearts is fourth best so declarer's king is the only one he has higher than the five.

Further, declarer has only three hearts, if not a doubleton, as he would have rebid one heart with four of them.

Besides the fact that we can grab five tricks, there is the danger that declarer can take nine if I duck this diamond.

I do take the diamond and cash the queen of hearts. Before taking the ten, I wonder if I should get greedy and switch to a spade.

Should I?

No. Just cash the ten of hearts. If partner has the ace of spades, he will let me win the ten of hearts and I will switch to spades. If he doesn't have the ace of spades, he will overtake the heart in order to cash out. There is no need for me to be clever.

I follow my thoughts and they lead to one down. Declarer had the hand I feared. This was no time for a diamond duck.

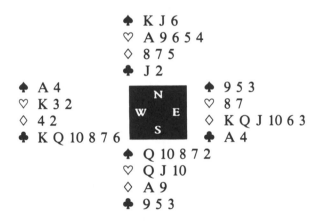

The rule of eleven is often maligned and sometimes justly so. But it is not without merit and here it made the defense easy.

FURTHER ANALYSIS

I played the heart jack rather than the ten so that if partner got in, he would not wonder if I had the QJ10 or the J10x.

Here is the problem from his point of view when I play the ten.

$\heartsuit$ 8 7

$\heartsuit$ A 9 6 5 4 $\heartsuit$ 10

$\heartsuit$ K

Looking at the heart suit in isolation partner, if he gets in, will not know whether to play another heart.

Are they

$\heartsuit$ 8 7

$\heartsuit$ A 9 6 5 4 $\heartsuit$ J 10 3

$\heartsuit$ K Q 2

Or

$\heartsuit$ 8 7

$\heartsuit$ A 9 6 5 4 $\heartsuit$ Q J 10

$\heartsuit$ K 3 2

In the first case, partner must switch and hope I can get in to return hearts.

In the second case, the hearts are running and we should get them going.

If, however, I play the jack from QJ10, partner will know that it is safe to lead another small heart. Either I have the QJx and we can run the suit or declarer has the KQ10, giving him a second stopper anyway.

58

♠ 8 7 2
♡ A 9 8
◇ 5 2
♣ Q 10 5 4 2

No one is vul. RHO and I both pass and LHO opens a third chair ONE SPADE. Partner overcalls TWO CLUBS and RHO bids TWO HEARTS. With such good support, it seems that I ought to raise, but it is unclear how high to go. Three clubs seems futile and five clubs excessive. In spite of my good clubs, I have terrible shape and don't want to punish partner if he has stepped out a little. I will content myself with a raise to FOUR CLUBS. We play this as preemptive in nature so if partner continues he will find me with a little extra.

LHO chooses to bid FOUR SPADES, but he doesn't seem overly sure of himself. When this is passed back to me I pass with no thought of bidding again.

Dealer: East
Vul: None

EAST	SOUTH	WEST	NORTH
Pass	Pass	1 ♠	2 ♣
2 ♡	4 ♣	4 ♠	Pass
Pass	Pass		

Partner begins with the king of clubs and I must decide whether to encourage.

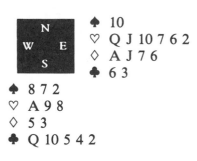

♠ 10
♡ Q J 10 7 6 2
◇ A J 7 6
♣ 6 3

♠ 8 7 2
♡ A 9 8
◇ 5 3
♣ Q 10 5 4 2

If I encourage, partner will continue clubs, declarer will ruff and he will either have four losers or he won't.

It's possible that my play to trick one won't matter. Declarer may ruff it. I'm going to assume, though, that the club will live. There are three reasons:

1. We probably need a club trick to beat four spades, so I will make the asumption that we have one.

2. Declarer might have had enough hearts to raise if he had a club void.

3. Partner, with six clubs, might have saved.

These reasons are hardly substantial, but in total they imply the club king will hold. Therefore I can assume that whatever message I choose to give, partner will be able to act on it.

I just thought of a fourth reason. Declarer, if void in clubs, might get tired of waiting for me to play. He might ruff in order to hurry things along. He hasn't done this.

Anyway, I still have to make up my mind.

Perhaps if I figure out what declarer has, I will be able to plan the defense.

I can begin by giving declarer one club at most. Also, he has six or more spades. With only five spades he would either have three hearts

5-3-4-1

and would prefer to raise hearts, or five diamonds,

5-2-5-1

and would bid four diamonds.

Therefore declarer is either 6-3-3-1 or 6-2-4-1. Unless, of course, he has more than six spades.

This makes it seem that a club continuation is unlikely to succeed.

Can a diamond switch be best?

This is likely only if partner has the king and queen of diamonds, and, if he does have them, then declarer will have the remaining high cards including the AKQ of spades and the heart

200

king.

Looking at declarer's possible shapes it appears that our best chance is to find partner with either:

1. A stiff heart plus a spade trick, or
2. Kx of hearts plus Jxx or better in spades.

Are these consistent with the bidding?
Let's see. Here are two possible layouts:

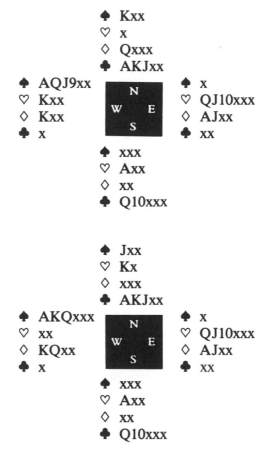

Both of these look reasonable. On the first setup, LHO might raise hearts instead, but four spades, while perhaps a bit hoggish, was not the worst bid ever.

The second hand is also possible. The queen of diamonds could be in partner's hand, but the general outline is okay. The two club bid by partner wasn't so hot, but then he does like to bid, so I don't think this construction is going to insult him.

If I am going to put all my eggs into one basket, I better be sure I can get partner into the same basket. I don't want to play the wrong club and have partner switch to diamonds.

Can I get partner to switch to hearts? Or is it impossible at this stage to do that?

I think I can do it. The theory is to play a peculiar card, which cannot have a normal meaning.

Will the ten do?

No. It falls into the category of normal signals. I would play that card in many situations where I wish to encouarge.

So?

So what's left is the queen. Partner will know I don't have the jack because he has it or declarer has it singleton. Therefore, he will view the queen as a most unusual card and should interpret it as calling for a heart switch.

I tend to think that he will not need any encouragement to switch to a stiff heart, but he might not be so enthusiastic about switching the Kx of hearts.

I do play the queen and partner is quick to play the king and another heart. A third round of hearts leads to down one.

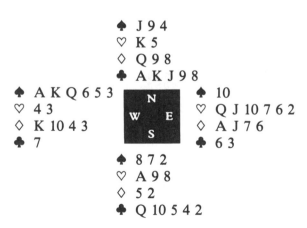

I see that the actual hand is almost exactly the same as my second hypothetical example.

FURTHER ANALYSIS

It is a common error to bid on with the South hand when the opponents reach four spades. In this instance it would be especially bad because partner has heard your bid and then expressed the opinion that he wants to defend against four spades. It would be antipartnership to overrule him.

Had the auction been different:

WEST	NORTH	EAST	SOUTH
		Pass	Pass
1 ♠	2 ♣	2 ♡	4 ♣
Pass	Pass	4 ♠	?

you could make a feeble case for five clubs on the theory that partner is now known to be short in spades, etc. I think it would still be poor to bid five clubs, but it is worse still on the actual auction where partner showed his preference for defense.

59

♠ 10 6 5 4
♡ A 10 3
◊ K J 7 6
♣ J 3

We are vulnerable against not and, having dealt, I pass. LHO opens ONE HEART and RHO's ONE NOTRUMP closes the auction.

Dealer: South
Vul: North-South

SOUTH	WEST	NORTH	EAST
Pass	1 ♡	Pass	1 NT
Pass	Pass	Pass	

This makes it my lead.

My two choices seem to be the four of spades or the six of diamonds. I am confident that one of these is my best lead but must decide which one.

In favor of diamonds is that they are much better than the spades. Against leading diamonds is the fact that RHO can have extremely good diamonds. He may have as good as AQ10xx, but not have been able to bid them.

In favor of spades is that RHO usually doesn't have good spades on this sequence. Against spades is that my partner could have bid them at the one level, if so inclined.

This is a typical decision based on nebulous and non-guaranteed facts. I choose the spade four and in my mind I make this a three to two favorite over diamonds. I'm quite prepared for it to be wrong.

The sight of dummy leaves me unsure which is best.

♠ A J 9
♡ Q J 8 6 5
◊ Q 8
♣ K 7 6

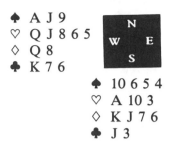

♠ 10 6 5 4
♡ A 10 3
◊ K J 7 6
♣ J 3

Dummy wins the jack, partner playing the two and declarer the seven. Dummy leads the five of hearts to partner's two and declarer's king, and I have to decide whether to take it.

Should I?

I think I will. Partner should give count in this situation so I can expect declarer to have another heart. But the real reason I am taking it is that we may be able to take a bunch of tricks.

Which tricks do I expect to take? Why?

On the auction, declarer ought not to have more than eight points I think he has.

It's possible he has the queen of clubs to go with his KQ of spades and the king of hearts, but it is likely that he doesn't have it. If so, we may be able to cash a larger number of minor suit tricks. If partner has the ten of clubs as well as the ace and queen (surely a small enough wish) we will be in business.

How should I proceed? Clubs or diamonds?

I think diamonds. We may have four tricks to cash there plus two club tricks. If I lead the club jack now, declarer may cover and partner will win. He might, if holding the AQ of clubs, underlead them to my ten. But I haven't got it. I don't think that if I lead the club jack partner should work out that I have this particular diamond holding. He does not know, as I do, that declarer has the KQ of spades.

I switch to the six of diamonds to partner's ace. He returns the nine to my king, felling dummy's queen.

I take the nine to mean he started with three diamonds or two. If he has three, then a club to partner and another diamond will cash out our four diamond tricks. But if partner has only two diamonds, I must cash out now and switch to the club jack hoping for the best. Can I tell?

No.

I am going to play the club jack on the theory that partner is more likely to have one more diamond than specifically the ten of clubs. The club jack is covered by the king and ace. The diamond five comes back and I get two more diamond tricks. Nice that the eight was in dummy. When I return the three of clubs, partner takes the queen and declarer the rest.

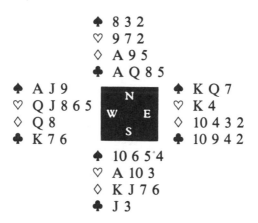

```
              ♠ 8 3 2
              ♡ 9 7 2
              ◊ A 9 5
              ♣ A Q 8 5
  ♠ A J 9           N        ♠ K Q 7
  ♡ Q J 8 6 5                ♡ K 4
  ◊ Q 8      W         E     ◊ 10 4 3 2
  ♣ K 7 6           S        ♣ 10 9 4 2
              ♠ 10 6 5 4
              ♡ A 10 3
              ◊ K J 7 6
              ♣ J 3
```

There were a number of inferences from both sides of the table. From my side the facts were reasonably clear. But from partner's side things were not as evident.

When partner took his ace of diamonds, it was easy to return the nine. But when I switched to the jack of clubs, partner had to decide whether to return his last diamond or play clubs. His final decision was based on a number of inferences:

1. I probably have four spades.
2. I surely have four diamonds.
3. I probably have three or more hearts else RHO would raise them rather than bid one notrump.
4. Thus I cannot have a third club.
5. If, by some chance, I did hold J10x of clubs, I could have chosen to shift to a club rather than a diamond from K10xx.

As with many defensive decisions, very little was black and white and solutions were based on a number of vague to fuzzy inferences.

FURTHER ANALYSIS

It might be tempting to lay down the king of diamonds after winning the heart ace. This will be effective most of the time, but will lose when partner has AQ10xx of clubs and the doubleton ace of diamonds.

Unless you suddenly change your mind!

60

♠ 10 2
♡ 7 3
◇ K 5 4 3 2
♣ Q J 8 3

With our side vul., my RHO opens ONE DIAMOND and
LHO responds ONE SPADE. Opener's ONE NOTRUMP
rebid is converted back to TWO SPADES by LHO and the auction ends.

Dealer: East
Vul: North-South

EAST	SOUTH	WEST	NORTH
1 ◇	Pass	1 ♠	Pass
1 NT	Pass	2 ♠	Pass
Pass	Pass		

Partner leads the queen of hearts and a mixed dummy comes
down.

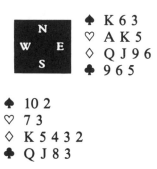

♠ K 6 3
♡ A K 5
◇ Q J 9 6
♣ 9 6 5

♠ 10 2
♡ 7 3
◇ K 5 4 3 2
♣ Q J 8 3

When dummy wins the king, I have to decide whether or not
to give count. I can make a case either way. If I think partner
will get in first, I ought to discourage because I don't want him
leading any more hearts unless his heart holding tells him to. I
don't want him leading hearts because I told him to.

On the flip side, if I get in first, it might be useful to have
given count so that when (if) I return the suit, partner will know

what's happening.

I play the three without conviction.

Declarer's next play, the six of diamonds, isn't quite the one I was expecting.

Normally I would expect declarer to draw some number of trumps and then lead diamonds towards the dummy.

What is going on in diamonds?

Almost certainly, declarer is not void in diamonds. Probably he has the ace or ten and is attempting to set up discards while keeping some entries to dummy.

Which diamond holding does he have?

Can't tell yet.

How about the rest of the hand?

This hand is a little odd from the point of view that dummy and I have only nineteen points. My partner couldn't act so declarer rates to have a decent hand.

Which high cards does partner have?

I know about the QJ of hearts and expect him to have one, but not both, club honors, else he would have led one. Perhaps he doesn't have either.

Where is the ace of diamonds?

I expect partner to have it. Declarer has a spade suit of some consequence, and at least one club honor. I tend to think he does not have the ace of diamonds.

How should the defense continue?

On the premise that partner has the ace of diamonds, I conclude that declarer has the ten, either singleton or doubleton. Since it is more productive for the defense to have me on lead, I rise with the king, excuses ready, and nervously await declarer's card. I'm confident, but not all that confident, and if declarer has the ace, I have made one serious error.

No, declarer plays the ten.

I switch to the queen of clubs and some good things happen. Declarer covers with the king losing to partner's ace. Partner cashes the ten and continues with the four to my jack, declarer following to all of these.

What now?

I could consider a diamond, but I think it more effective to return a heart. If declarer has six spades, the heart return may prevent partner from being squeezed in hearts and diamonds, and if declarer has five spades, I won't be setting up the diamonds for two heart discards.

My heart seven goes to partner's eight and dummy's ace. Declarer calls for the queen of diamonds and I duck perforce. Declarer, not knowing if I am ducking or just following suit, finally elects to pitch a heart. Partner wins the ace of diamonds, cashes the jack of hearts, and leads the nine of hearts. By now, all the hearts have been played, declarer having started with 10642. Dummy discards the nine of diamonds. Since my partner wants me to uppercut for him, I do so with the ten of spades. Declarer beats this with the queen and after some thought leads the nine for a finesse. This negates our uppercut and holds the set to one trick.

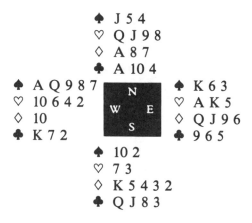

```
              ♠ J 5 4
              ♡ Q J 9 8
              ◊ A 8 7
              ♣ A 10 4
  ♠ A Q 9 8 7       ♠ K 6 3
  ♡ 10 6 4 2        ♡ A K 5
  ◊ 10              ◊ Q J 9 6
  ♣ K 7 2          ♣ 9 6 5
              ♠ 10 2
              ♡ 7 3
              ◊ K 5 4 3 2
              ♣ Q J 8 3
```

Although the end game was amusing, the main point of this hand is the play of the diamond king. Its effect is best appreciated when you see the result of not playing it.

◊ QJ96

◊ A87   ◊ K5432

◊ 10

If East ducks the six of diamonds, the ten forces the ace. Subsequently, the queen is led. If East covers, it is ruffed and two discards are available. This results in declarer's winning nine tricks rather than seven. Declarer might actually come to ten tricks if West makes a hasty shift to clubs. This would set up declarer's king.

61

♠ 8 7 4 3
♡ 7
♢ A Q 9
♣ Q 10 6 4 2

We are vul vs vul against a pair that bids a lot. LHO opens
ONE HEART and RHO responds ONE SPADE. It looks like it
may be their hand and the auction confirms it. Opener rebids
TWO HEARTS and when raised to THREE HEARTS he finds
enough to bid FOUR HEARTS. The way this pair bids, I sometimes wonder if they look at their cards. We will find out.

Dealer: West
Vul: North-South

WEST	NORTH	EAST	NORTH
1 ♡	Pass	1 ♠	Pass
2 ♡	Pass	3 ♡	Pass
4 ♡	Pass	Pass	Pass

Partner leads the ten of hearts and it seems that dummy, at
least, has full values.

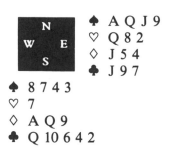

♠ A Q J 9
♡ Q 8 2
♢ J 5 4
♣ J 9 7

♠ 8 7 4 3
♡ 7
♢ A Q 9
♣ Q 10 6 4 2

Declarer wins the lead in hand with the king. Next he leads
the ten of spades to the ace and returns the queen.
   What's up?
   Declarer has a stiff spade and intends to take a ruffing
finesse. When I do not produce the king, declarer will take a
discard now and two more later after drawing trump.

Who has the high cards?
Partner has the spade king.
Declarer has the AKJ of hearts either six or seven times.
Declarer has a club honor else partner would have led one from the AK.
Partner may or may not have the king of diamonds.
How should the defense proceed?
Since we cannot beat this hand if partner hasn't got the king of diamonds, I am going to assume he has it. If so, I want him to lead diamonds rather than clubs when he gets his king of spades.
Can I arrange this?
I think so. By playing my spades 4-8 it will appear that I am going out of my way to ask for something. Partner should interpret this as a request for diamonds.
On the queen of spades, declarer sheds the three of clubs. Partner wins the king and spends a bit of time looking at that club.
I will him to look at my cards, not declarer's cards. This is hard work, but it succeeds. Partner exits with the three of diamonds and we are able to cash three tricks.

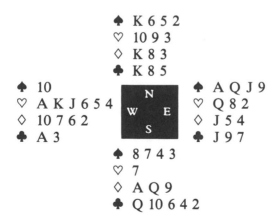

```
              ♠ K 6 5 2
              ♡ 10 9 3
              ◇ K 8 3
              ♣ K 8 5
  ♠ 10                        ♠ A Q J 9
  ♡ A K J 6 5 4    N          ♡ Q 8 2
  ◇ 10 7 6 2    W     E       ◇ J 5 4
  ♣ A 3           S           ♣ J 9 7
              ♠ 8 7 4 3
              ♡ 7
              ◇ A Q 9
              ♣ Q 10 6 4 2
```

Declarer's play was well conceived. By playing spades right away, he prevented me from making a useful discard. Fortunately, it was possible to overcome this via the suit preference signal.

Note that in this particular situation, my exact spade holding is known to partner. And I know he knows it. Theoretically, I have twelve ways to play to the first two spade tricks. It would seem that I ought to be able to get quite a few messages across.

As it is, I can clearly get a diamond lead, but have no defined way to get a club lead except by the inference that I didn't request a diamond.

It would be useful for a partnership to have understandings as to the difference between what 3-4 would mean as opposed to 4-3, given that the holding is known to be 8743.

For instance. Does 3-8 say I kind of like diamonds? Does 7-8 say I love diamonds? I don't have any answers, but it must be worth looking at.

62

♠ 10 9 7 5
♡ Q J 6 2
◊ 10 9 3
♣ J 2

We are not vul vs vul. When my RHO opens ONE NO-TRUMP, my LHO sits up and looks very interested. It is evident that this is not our hand.

Partner and I are able to relax for a while while our opponents conduct one of the longer auctions I can remember,

Dealer: East
Vul: East-West

EAST	SOUTH	WEST	NORTH
1 NT	Pass	2 ◊ *	Pass
2 ♡	Pass	3 ♣	Pass
3 ♡	Pass	3 ♠	Pass
4 ♣	Pass	4 ◊	Pass
4 ♠	Pass	4 NT	Pass
5 ♡ *	Pass	5 NT	Pass
6 ◊ *	Pass	6 ♡	Pass
Pass	Pass		

*Alerts

We sort out that it is my lead. Before doing do, I get a review and ascertain that:

1. Two diamonds was a transfer to hearts.
2. Three clubs was natural.
3. Three hearts was a good hand for hearts.

Then there was some cue bidding before Blackwood. RHO's answers showed two aces and either the king or queen of trump.

My hand shows some promise. Their trumps are Axxxx in LHO's hand and Kxx in RHO's with the possibility of either having an additional trump so I have at least one trump trick.

What should I lead?

From the auction, it sounds like the opponents have no losers in spades or diamonds, so there is no rush to lead either to establish the setting trick. Likely, the setting trick will come from hearts or clubs if partner has the queen.

Perhaps I should simply lead a spade or a diamond as a safe lead and hope for the best. It is certainly tempting.

Is it also best?

I'm not sure. I can envision approximately how the play will go. Declarer will win the opening lead and, if his hand is solid as I envision it, he will conclude that only a bad trump break will defeat him. He will end up taking some form of safety play which will prove to be necessary.

So what is there to do about it?

What I can do about it is perhaps talk declarer out of it. If I lead a club, declarer may fear a club ruff and give up on the safety play.

Is this not dangerous? Could not partner have the queen of clubs? This club lead could cost us a club trick, perhaps the setting trick.

I don't think this is likely. LHO was trying for seven so I think it reasonable to assume he wasn't worried about a club loser.

In any event, I think the club lead has so much to gain that the risk can be ignored. I'm going to lead a club. And since my thumb is nearest the two, I select it.

It works. The play takes about ten agonzied seconds.

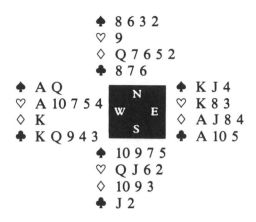

```
              ♠ 8 6 3 2
              ♡ 9
              ◇ Q 7 6 5 2
              ♣ 8 7 6
♠ A Q           ┌───────┐        ♠ K J 4
♡ A 10 7 5 4    │   N   │        ♡ K 8 3
◇ K             │ W   E │        ◇ A J 8 4
♣ K Q 9 4 3     │   S   │        ♣ A 10 5
                └───────┘
              ♠ 10 9 7 5
              ♡ Q J 6 2
              ◇ 10 9 3
              ♣ J 2
```

Declarer wins the ten and plays the king and ace of hearts.

FURTHER ANALYSIS

Declarer might have suspected what was going on, but given the obvious paucity of good leads, South might easily choose to lead a stiff club, even given that the suit had been bid and raised (sort of). It was not hard to believe that the two was stiff.

63

♠ A 6 4
♡ A J 10 7 3
◇ 9 2
♣ 10 4 3

Our opponents are vulnerable and my RHO opens ONE CLUB. For a change, I can contest and try ONE HEART. LHO bids ONE SPADE and my partner raises to TWO HEARTS. When RHO bids TWO SPADES, I can find no reason to persist and pass. LHO makes a game try with THREE CLUBS and RHO shows signs of life with THREE DIAMONDS. My LHO jumps to FOUR SPADES which completes the auction.

Dealer: East
Vul: East-West

EAST	SOUTH	WEST	NORTH
1 ♣	1 ♡	1 ♠	2 ♡
2 ♠	Pass	3 ♣	Pass
3 ◇	Pass	4 ♠	Pass
Pass	Pass		

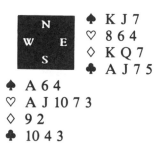

♠ K J 7
♡ 8 6 4
◇ K Q 7
♣ A J 7 5

♠ A 6 4
♡ A J 10 7 3
◇ 9 2
♣ 10 4 3

My partner leads the king of hearts and declarer thinks for a moment before playing. While he's thinking, I look at the dummy and think that it was a difficult hand to bid. Well handled. When declarer finally plays the four I have to consider my options.

One of them is to overtake and return a diamond. Perhaps we have a ruff coming.

Not likely. For this to be correct, declarer would have to have a stiff heart and three little diamonds. This would leave the spade queen and the club KQ as his assets. Also, my partner would have had more to say.

I can do no more than encourage with the seven. Partner continues with the queen and I overtake to lead the jack. Declarer follows to two hearts and ruffs the third with the ten of spades. Next comes the spade two to partner's five and dummy's king.

Do I take my ace now or later?

If I take it, where will the setting trick come from?

One place is the club suit. If declarer has Qxx of clubs, we will have a club trick coming.

Is this likely?

Not too likely. That would leave declarer with

♠ Q10xxx
♡ xx
♢ AJx
♣ Qxx.

I think it more likely that declarer has the club king or KQ and, in either case, we have no club trick coming as long as declarer plays the hand sensibly.

Is there any other possible source of a fourth trick?

Yes. The possibility exists that declarer has only four spades.

How can I take advantage of this?

With only four spades, declarer will not be able to draw trump if I do not relase my ace. The plan will be to duck this trick and the next as well. If declarer started with a four bagger, he is down to three trumps. After two leads he will be down to one, as will everyone else at the table. Now if he leads another trump I can take it and will have two good hearts to cash. If declarer leaves trumps alone now, my partner will be able to ruff a club whenever declarer has four clubs.

I think this is a reasonable thing to play for. It's certainly way ahead of whatever is in second place.

When I duck the spade king, declarer leads the seven to his nine which wins, my partner completing an echo with the three.

This defense may work if declarer started with only four trumps.

If declarer has only three clubs, he can overcome by cashing three clubs and then leading diamonds, but if he has four clubs, he is stuck.

Declarer turns out to have 4-2-3-4 so this defense is effective. Declarer elects to lead clubs and my partner gets a ruff for one down.

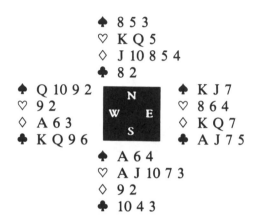

         ♠ 8 5 3
         ♡ K Q 5
         ◇ J 10 8 5 4
         ♣ 8 2

♠ Q 10 9 2   ♠ K J 7
♡ 9 2   ♡ 8 6 4
◇ A 6 3   ◇ K Q 7
♣ K Q 9 6   ♣ A J 7 5

         ♠ A 6 4
         ♡ A J 10 7 3
         ◇ 9 2
         ♣ 10 4 3

I note that the four-three spade fit is the only game that has a chance.

FURTHER ANALYSIS

Partner's trump echo was a comfort. Even though I would have defended this way without it, it was nice to know in advance. This is in keeping with my idea that a trump echo should be given whenever it won't give away the trump suit. The information may be of use to partner in some peculiar ways.

64

♠ 4
♡ J 10 5
◇ A J 6 2
♣ J 10 9 5 2

No one is vulnerable and LHO opens ONE CLUB. RHO responds ONE SPADE over which opener jumps to TWO NO-TRUMP. RHO rebids his spades and LHO raises to FOUR SPADES.

Dealer: West
Vul: None

WEST	NORTH	EAST	SOUTH
1 ♣	Pass	1 ♠	Pass
2 NT	Pass	3 ♠	Pass
4 ♠	Pass	Pass	Pass

With clubs bid on my left, I choose the slightly more dangerous, but more aggressive lead of the heart jack over the club jack.

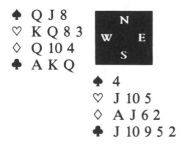

♠ Q J 8
♡ K Q 8 3
◇ Q 10 4
♣ A K Q

♠ 4
♡ J 10 5
◇ A J 6 2
♣ J 10 9 5 2

My lead is covered by the king and won by partner's ace. Partner returns the heart two which goes to my ten and the queen. Declarer has followed twice with the four and six.

Where are the missing hearts?

I expect partner has them, although it is possible that declarer does. What is clear is that someone has both the seven and nine of hearts; they are not divided.

The queen of spades is led, winning, and the eight is led to declarer's nine. Partner has played up the line in spades, with the three and five.

Declarer leads the eight of diamonds.

What's this about. Should I take it or should I make a seemingly normal duck?

How can I tell?

I check the various cases.

First, if declarer has seven spades, then he may be attempting to sneak a diamond trick through before pitching his other diamond on a club.

```
♠ AKxxxxx
♡ xx
◇ Kx
♣ xx
```

I think this unlikely because declarer would still be bidding.

If declarer has six spades, then it doesn't matter what I do in diamonds.

Say declarer has

```
♠ K10xxxx
♡ xx
◇ Kxxx
♣ x
```

We have only one diamond trick in any case.

What if declarer has five spades?

Can our diamond trick go away?

No.

Should I duck hoping declarer has K9xx of diamonds and misguesses?

Perhaps. But there is a more promising defense.

What is that?

If declarer has only five spades, we may be able to beat him by adopting a forcing game. If declarer can be made to ruff twice, my partner will have more trumps than declarer. If I duck the diamond, partner will win the king (hypothetical) when declarer finesses the ten. Partner will be able to tap declarer only once because he will have to lead the nine of hearts to do it. This will establish dummy's eight so we can't tap him a second time. Of course, partner could underlead the nine but

1. Declarer might have the missing heart.
2. Declarer might let it run to dummy's eight out of desperation.

But I don't have to give partner that option. By rising with the ace of diamonds, and leading my last heart, we will be able to tap declarer and still maintain heart control.

This seems to be a solid choice so I do rise with the ace and continue hearts. Declarer ruffs, draws trump and leads a diamond, finessing the ten. The finesse wins, but partner produces the missing heart for one down.

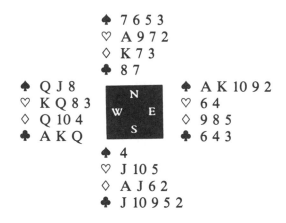

                        ♠ 7 6 5 3
                        ♡ A 9 7 2
                        ◇ K 7 3
                        ♣ 8 7
    ♠ Q J 8   ♠ A K 10 9 2
    ♡ K Q 8 3   N   ♡ 6 4
    ◇ Q 10 4   W   E   ◇ 9 8 5
    ♣ A K Q   S   ♣ 6 4 3
                        ♠ 4
                        ♡ J 10 5
                        ◇ A J 6 2
                        ♣ J 10 9 5 2

I note that three notrump is cold. Next time perhaps, East will be less anxious to show his five bagger.

FURTHER ANALYSIS

Grabbing the diamond ace is the winning play in the actual hand and it would also have been the winning play if partner had held the ace fourth of spades and no king of diamonds.

65

♠ K 2
♡ Q J 4
◇ J 7 6 3
♣ A 10 7 2

With only our opponents vulnerable, my LHO opens ONE HEART. Partner makes a skip bid warning and bids TWO SPADES. RHO waits a reasonable length of time and raises to THREE HEARTS. My choices are to pass or to raise to three spades. I choose to raise to THREE SPADES for a number of reasons, although none of them are too solid.

I have a little defense against four hearts, so I won't be unhappy if they bid it.

Our weak jump overcalls are not as atrocious as some, so my hand won't be an enormous disappointment. We could go for three hundred but that would require that they double us and then beat us two.

And lastly, I would like partner to lead spades.

LHO continues to FOUR HEARTS and all pass.

Dealer: West
Vul: East-West

WEST	NORTH	EAST	SOUTH
1 ♡	2 ♠	3 ♡	3 ♠
4 ♡	Pass	Pass	Pass

Partner, in response to my raise, leads the ten of diamonds. So much for my three spade bid.

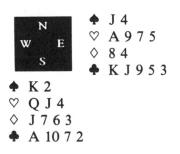

♠ J 4
♡ A 9 7 5
◇ 8 4
♣ K J 9 5 3

♠ K 2
♡ Q J 4
◇ J 7 6 3
♣ A 10 7 2

What's going on? Why didn't partner lead a spade?

Normally there are two or three possible reasons why partner doesn't lead the suit you have raised.

One reason is that he has a good holding in another suit such as KQJ or AKJ. On this hand, this is not the reason.

Another possibility is that the opening leader has a stiff. Again, this does not seem to apply here.

And finally, partner's holding in the suit your side has bid may be headed by the ace and he may wish not to start that suit, my raise notwithstanding.

This final reason seems to be the only one which might hold on this hand. This information is of no immediate value, but on some hands, it is. Perhaps it will become pertinent on this one.

In the meantime, declarer is pretty happy with this lead. He wins his queen and plays to the heart ace and back to his king, my partner following small and then discarding the eight of spades.

Declarer, still happy, cashes two more high diamonds, pitching one of dummy's spades. My partner follows to these with the five and nine.

Now declarer bangs down the queen of clubs. Partner plays the four, dummy the three.

I wish partner had led a spade. The defense would have been much faster and it would have been effective. Now I wonder if we can still beat four hearts.

Can we? What do I know thus far?

At this stage I can be pretty sure declarer is 3-5-4-1. Our jump overcalls usually show six card suits. This accounts for the three spades. Declarer has shown five hearts. And partner's play in diamonds certainly looks like three. All this, plus partner's four of clubs points to declarer's being 3-5-4-1.

This was easy. What do I do with it? Should I take the queen of clubs or should I let declarer have it?

Taking it provides declarer a clear route to ten tricks. That won't work. I'll have to consider what happens if I duck. Will declarer be able to come to ten tricks in a different fashion? Can he get some additional ruffs in dummy? Can he still set up the club suit?

I don't think so. If I duck, declarer can ruff a diamond and lead the club king for a ruffing finesse. This will set up a club

225

trick, but he won't have an entry to use it. I will be able to get in with the king of spades, cash my trump, and then, maybe, cash two more spades as well. The play goes as anticipated. I duck the queen of clubs and declarer, who obviously overlooked this twist, loses some of his enthusiasm. The ultimate result is one down when partner's spades turn out to sufficiently strong.

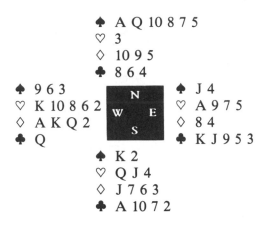

        ♠ A Q 10 8 7 5
        ♡ 3
        ◇ 10 9 5
        ♣ 8 6 4
♠ 9 6 3   ♠ J 4
♡ K 10 8 6 2   ♡ A 9 7 5
◇ A K Q 2   ◇ 8 4
♣ Q   ♣ K J 9 5 3
        ♠ K 2
        ♡ Q J 4
        ◇ J 7 6 3
        ♣ A 10 7 2

Declarer timed the hand rather poorly. He could have made it in a number of ways. He could have played off three diamonds early, or he could have played off the king of hearts and then led diamonds. It is true that either of these lines could lose an overtrick, but the contract is a good one and an overtrick should be of less consequence than making the contract.

At matchpoints, declarer's line has a little to be said for it, but at IMP's or rubber bridge, the line is a bit soft.

Of course, if declarer thought that the diamonds were six-one, then the line has more to recommend it. In any event, the defensive problem as it actually came up is a good one.

50 HIGHLY-RECOMMENDED TITLES

**CALL TOLL FREE 1-800-274-2221
IN THE U.S. & CANADA TO ORDER ANY OF
THEM OR TO REQUEST OUR
FULL-COLOR 64 PAGE CATALOG OF
ALL BRIDGE BOOKS IN PRINT,
SUPPLIES AND GIFTS.**

FOR BEGINNERS
#0300 Future Champions' Bridge Series
#2130 Kantar-Introduction to Declarer's Play
#2135 Kantar-Introduction to Defender's Play
#1121 Silverman-Elementary Bridge
       Five Card Major Student Text
#0660 Penick-Beginning Bridge Complete
#0661 Penick-Beginning Bridge Quizzes
#3230 Lampert-Fun Way to Serious Bridge

FOR ADVANCED PLAYERS
#0740 Woolsey-Matchpoints
#0741 Woolsey-Partnership Defense
#1702 Bergen-Competitive Auctions

BIDDING — 2 OVER 1 GAME FORCE
#4750 Bruno & Hardy-Two-Over-One Game Force:
       An Introduction
#1750 Hardy-Two-Over-One Game Force
#1790 Lawrence-Workbook on the Two Over One System
#4525 Lawrence-Bidding Quizzes Book 1

DEFENSE
#0520 Blackwood-Complete Book of Opening Leads
#0631 Lawrence-Dynamic Defense
#1200 Woolsey-Modern Defensive Signalling

FOR INTERMEDIATE PLAYERS
#3015 Root-Commonsense Bidding
#0630 Lawrence-Card Combinations
#0102 Stewart-Baron-The Bridge Book 2
#1122 Silverman-Intermediate Bridge Five
      Card Major Student Text
#0575 Lampert-The Fun Way to Advanced Bridge
#0633 Lawrence-How to Read Your Opponents' Cards
#3672 Truscott-Bid Better, Play Better
#1765 Lawrence-Judgment at Bridge

PLAY OF THE HAND
#2150 Kantar-Test your Bridge Play, Vol. 1
#3675 Watson-Watson's Classic Book on
      the Play of the Hand
#3009 Root-How to Play a Bridge Hand
#1124 Silverman-Play of the Hand as
      Declarer and Defender
#2175 Truscott-Winning Declarer Play
#3803 Sydnor-Bridge Made Easy Book 3

CONVENTIONS
#2115 Kantar-Bridge Conventions
#3011 Root-Pavlicek-Modern Bridge Conventions
#0240 Championship Bridge Series (All 36)

DUPLICATE STRATEGY
#2260 Sheinwold-Duplicate Bridge
#2800 Granovetter-Conventions at a Glance
#1750 Hardy-2 Over 1 Game Force
#2038 Seagram-25 Bridge Conventions You Should Know

FOR ALL PLAYERS
#3889 Darvas & de V. Hart-Right Through The Pack
#0790 Simon- Why You Lose at Bridge

Andersen THE LEBENSOHL CONVENTION COMPLETE
Baron THE BRIDGE PLAYER'S DICTIONARY
Blackwood COMPLETE BOOK OF OPENING LEADS
Boeder THINKING ABOUT IMPS
Bruno-Hardy 2 OVER 1 GAME FORCE: AN INTRODUCTION
Darvas & De V. Hart RIGHT THROUGH THE PACK
Grant

    BRIDGE BASICS 1: AN INTRODUCTION
    BRIDGE BASICS 2: COMPETITIVE BIDDING
    BRIDGE BASICS 3: POPULAR CONVENTIONS
    BRIDGE AT A GLANCE
    IMPROVING YOUR JUDGMENT: OPENING THE BIDDING
    IMPROVING YOUR JUDGMENT: DOUBLES
Groner DUPLICATE BRIDGE DIRECTION
Hardy
    TWO-OVER-ONE GAME FORCE
    TWO-OVER-ONE GAME FORCE QUIZ BOOK
Harris BRIDGE DIRECTOR'S COMPANION (5th Edition)
Kay COMPLETE BOOK OF DUPLICATE BRIDGE
Kelsey THE TRICKY GAME
Lampert THE FUN WAY TO ADVANCED BRIDGE
Lawrence
    CARD COMBINATIONS
    COMPLETE BOOK ON BALANCING
    DYNAMIC DEFENSE
    HOW TO READ YOUR OPPONENTS' CARDS
    JUDGMENT AT BRIDGE
    PARTNERSHIP UNDERSTANDINGS
    PLAY BRIDGE WITH MIKE LAWRENCE
    PLAY SWISS TEAMS WITH MIKE LAWRENCE
    WORKBOOK ON THE TWO OVER ONE SYSTEM
Lipkin INVITATION TO ANNIHILATION
Penick
    BEGINNING BRIDGE COMPLETE
    BEGINNING BRIDGE QUIZZES
Rosenkranz
    BRIDGE: THE BIDDER'S GAME
    TIPS FOR TOPS
    MORE TIPS FOR TOPS
    TRUMP LEADS
    OUR MAN GODFREY
Rosenkranz & Alder BID TO WIN, PLAY FOR PLEASURE
Rosenkranz & Truscott BIDDING ON TARGET
Simon
    WHY YOU LOSE AT BRIDGE
Thomas SHERLOCK HOLMES, BRIDGE DETECTIVE
Woolsey
    MATCHPOINTS
    MODERN DEFENSIVE SIGNALLING
    PARTNERSHIP DEFENSE
World Bridge Federation APPEALS COMMITTEE DECISIONS
    from the 1994 NEC WORLD CHAMPIONSHIPS